A More Promising Musical Future

Today's higher education music faculty and administrators are faced with extraordinary pressure to adapt, innovate, and change. But what change is most critical to pursue – and how can it be brought about effectively? This concise volume brings together four seasoned thought leaders with distinct voices, each providing a complimentary glimpse into how music faculty and administrators can help lead changes that truly matter. Making the case for transformations to better align music training in higher education with our culturally diverse society and the actual marketplace facing graduates, the perspectives collected here provide essential change management leadership strategies for music departments in the 21st century.

Covering topics such as diversity and inclusion, institutional transformation, and preparing students for contemporary music careers, each chapter includes an outline of specific steps that can be taken individually and collectively towards needed change. Illuminating issues and providing practical suggestions, this book will enable both music faculty and administrators to confidently navigate change together with their communities.

Michael Stepniak is Dean and Professor of Music at Shenandoah Conservatory of Shenandoah University.

CMS Emerging Fields in Music
Series Editor: Mark Rabideau, University of Colorado, Denver, USA
Managing Editor: Zoua Sylvia Yang, DePauw University, USA

The *CMS Series in Emerging Fields in Music* consists of concise monographs that help the profession re-imagine how we must prepare 21st Century Musicians. Shifting cultural landscapes, emerging technologies, and a changing profession in-and-out of the academy demand that we re-examine our relationships with audiences, leverage our art to strengthen the communities in which we live and work, equip our students to think and act as artist-entrepreneurs, explore the limitless (and sometimes limiting) role technology plays in the life of a musician, revisit our very assumptions about what artistic excellence means and how personal creativity must be repositioned at the center of this definition, and share best practices and our own stories of successes and failures when leading institutional change.

These short-form books can be either single-authored works, or contributed volumes comprised of 3 or 4 essays on related topics. The books should prove useful for emerging musicians inventing the future they hope to inhabit, faculty rethinking the courses they teach and how they teach them, and administrators guiding curricular innovation and rebranding institutional identity.

Music as Care
Artistry in the Hospital Environment: CMS Emerging Fields in Music
Sarah Hoover

A More Promising Musical Future
Leading Transformational Change in Music Higher Education
Edited by Michael Stepniak

For more information, please visit: https://www.routledge.com/CMS-Emerging-Fields-in-Music/book-series/CMSEMR

A More Promising Musical Future

Leading Transformational Change in Music Higher Education

**Edited by
Michael Stepniak**

First published 2023
by Routledge
605 Third Avenue, New York, NY 10158

and by Routledge
4 Park Square, Milton Park, Abingdon, Oxon, OX14 4RN

Routledge is an imprint of the Taylor & Francis Group, an informa business

© 2023 selection and editorial matter, Michael Stepniak; individual chapters, the contributors

The right of Michael Stepniak to be identified as the author of the editorial material, and of the author for their individual chapters, has been asserted in accordance with sections 77 and 78 of the Copyright, Designs and Patents Act 1988.

All rights reserved. No part of this book may be reprinted or reproduced or utilised in any form or by any electronic, mechanical, or other means, now known or hereafter invented, including photocopying and recording, or in any information storage or retrieval system, without permission in writing from the publishers.

Trademark notice: Product or corporate names may be trademarks or registered trademarks, and are used only for identification and explanation without intent to infringe.

Library of Congress Cataloging-in-Publication Data
Names: Stepniak, Michael, editor.
Title: A more promising musical future: leading transformational change in music higher education/[edited by] Michael Stepniak.
Description: [1.] | New York: Routledge, 2022. | Series: CMS emerging fields in music.
Identifiers: LCCN 2022015540 (print) | LCCN 2022015541 (ebook) | ISBN 9781032111513 (hardback) | ISBN 9781032111520 (paperback) | ISBN 9781003218630 (ebook)
Subjects: LCSH: Music–Instruction and study. | Education, Higher. | Curriculum change. | Culturally relevant pedagogy. | Music–Vocational guidance.
Classification: LCC MT18 .M67 2022 (print) | LCC MT18 (ebook) | DDC 780.71–dc23/eng/20220401
LC record available at https://lccn.loc.gov/2022015540
LC ebook record available at https://lccn.loc.gov/2022015541

ISBN: 978-1-032-11151-3 (hbk)
ISBN: 978-1-032-11152-0 (pbk)
ISBN: 978-1-003-21863-0 (ebk)

DOI: 10.4324/9781003218630

Typeset in Times New Roman
by KnowledgeWorks Global Ltd.

Contents

List of Figures and Tables	vi
Series Editor's Introduction	vii
Preface	ix

1 **Changing the Game for Music in Higher Education**   1
   DAVID CUTLER

2 **Transforming Community and Ourselves through Heart and Mind Work: A Pathway for Embracing Diversity, Inclusion, Equity, Belonging, and Justice**   37
   JASMINE D. PARKER

3 **Embracing The 21st Century Superpowers of Creativity, Collaboration, Entrepreneurship, Adaptability, and Playfulness**   62
   BRIAN PERTL

4 **Readying Our Classical Music Performers – An Employer's View**   86
   KENDRA WHITLOCK INGRAM

Index   105

List of Figures and Tables

Figure

1.1 Curriculum Gameboard from Carolina/College Music
     Society Summit 2.0   20

Table

4.1 Music Industry Experts Interviewed   91

Series Editor's Introduction

Music is embraced throughout every culture without boundaries. Today, an increasingly connected world offers influence and inspiration for opening our imaginations, as technology provides unprecedented access to global audiences. Communities gather around music to mourn collective hardships and celebrate shared moments, and every parent understands that music enhances their child's chances to succeed in life. Yet it has never been more of a struggle for musicians to make a living at their art – at least when following traditional paths.

The College Music Society's *Emerging Fields in Music Series* champions the search for solutions to the most pressing challenges and most influential opportunities presented to the music profession during this time of uncertainty and promise. This series re-examines how we as music professionals can build relationships with audiences, leverage our art to strengthen the communities in which we live and work, equip our students to think and act as artist-entrepreneurs, explore the limitless (and sometimes limiting) role technology plays in the creation and dissemination of music, revisit our very assumptions about what artistic excellence means, and share best practices and our own stories of successes and failures when leading institutional change.

The world and the profession are changing. And so must we, if we are to carry forward our most beloved traditions of the past and create an audience for our best future.

Leading Change in a time of uncertainty and promise (a collection within the series) offers a comprehensive scaffolding of *why, what, how,* and *for whom* meaningful change is necessary if music schools are to equip students to invent the future they will soon inherit, offer faculty insights for rethinking the courses they teach and how they teach them, and recalibrate administrators' priorities, policies, and procedures as they paint the new landscape of the 21st century music school. The editor's premise for the collection is that institutions of higher learning in music must see their principal role as one that prepares musicians as one-of-a-kind artists-to-the-world, equipped with the requisite knowledge, skills, and understandings to create a lifetime of artistic moments, one after the next.

The collection begins by making the argument for music's "essential" place within the human experience as the foundation of professional and career development. It then offers and examines pillars for change by addressing three fundamental questions facing the profession:

> Pillar 1: Whose music matters?

> Pillar 2: What might be possible if we were to reposition creativity at the center of all that we do?

> Pillar 3: How might individuals and communities, through the work of career musicians and the experience of music, become more joyful, hopeful, connected, and healthy through musical experience?

Each pillar opens with an anchor manuscript that provides a comprehensive approach for imagining change. Subsequent books within each pillar offer specific ways forward.

Finally, three books examine *how* the systems and eco-systems that drive our music schools maintain inequities and obstruct innovation. Examining the academic journeys of students, faculty, and administrators, the authors decode often invisible systems that limit our growth and offer opportunities to realign our words and actions with the goals of fighting for equity, fostering inclusivity, celebrating creativity, and embracing community and the joy inherent within music-making.

This book guides readers on a personal journey toward fostering more authentic and inclusive cultures within their departments and schools. Invigorated by the human potential of our music communities, and the future of the music marketplace, it offers insight into change management and lays out practical pathways towards innovation and progress.

Preface

The 21st century continues to careen along, with extraordinary social, technological, and political change happening all around us. Amidst swirling change, higher education faces a growing existential crisis as the general public increasingly questions its cost and value. Simultaneously, our society is navigating a time of racial reckoning. Values such as civility and beauty - values that previously guided much inquiry and practice within academe – are now tarnished, aligned as they are with the continuation of the status quo. In the field of the performing arts, there continues to be a revolution in all aspects of the marketplace. Everything seems in flux, from the platforms used to reach audiences to how careers of performers are developed and what traditions are in or out of favor. Not surprisingly, music faculty and administrators are faced with extraordinary pressure to adapt, innovate, and change. But what change is critical to pursue, and how might it be best pursued?

This monograph brings together four seasoned thought leaders with four distinct voices, each providing a complimentary glimpse into how individual faculty and administrators can pursue and help lead changes that truly matter. The aim of the volume is straightforward; to both illuminate issues and provide practical suggestions. Each chapter, therefore, includes an outline of specific steps that might be taken individually and collectively towards needed change.

In the first chapter, David Cutler, one of the leading champions of entrepreneurship within music in higher education, sets the stage and directly tackles the very concept of change within higher education communities. Beyond outlining 5 critical questions that music faculty and administrators should ask as they and their communities navigate any significant change, he outlines a richly designed framework for how a community – however small or large - can identify actionable tactics that can lead to institutional transformation.

In the second chapter, Jasmine Parker, formerly of Berklee College of Music and now the Senior Director of Equity and Inclusion at Dallas College, outlines the need for our music communities to embrace and embody the values of diversity, inclusion, equity, belonging, and justice. She explains that the work of making a community more inclusive and equitable begins with very personal work. As Parker outlines, music faculty and administrators must each engage in specific heart and mind work and further develop their own emotional intelligence. As she explains, careful heart and mind work creates space for the synergistic exchange of thoughts, feelings, viewpoints, and ideas between all members of a community. It is through this work – which must begin at the individual faculty member level – that a community can enhance student performance outcomes as students increasingly feel safe while learning, exploring, and creating.

In the third chapter, longtime conservatory dean Brian Pertl tackles one of the oddities in higher education. Namely, the monumental disconnect that exists between the true needs of an ideal 21st century musician and the nature of the institutions tasked with giving our music students the skills aligned with those needs. Beyond questioning the unchanging model of training provided by Western classical music schools and programs, he proposes a new model; one that places creativity, entrepreneurship, collaboration, adaptability, and playfulness at its core. Not surprisingly, Pertl argues that we each need to become the creative, entrepreneurial, collaborative, adaptable, and playful problem-solvers we aspire to foster.

In the fourth and final chapter, noted arts presenter Kendra Ingram digs further into the practical issues of what graduates of music performance programs need to 'book the gig.' After further investigating and delineating the rapidly changing work environment facing music performance graduates, Ingram offers insights gleaned in part from her conversation with fellow music industry experts. Those insights are collected under three themes: (a) the importance of developing musicians who can engage and collaborate; (b) the need for greater emphasis on professional development and employment skill building and (c) the need for holistic education, with an emphasis on developing a well-rounded graduate. She concludes by reflecting on how a global pandemic and America's racial reckoning will affect the next generation of professional performing musicians.

In the end, this monograph is offered with the hope that music faculty and administrators may find it as a useful reference when they further consider how to pursue change that truly matters within their institutions. There are many nuggets that may be of value here to faculty leaders and administrators. If but two or three powerfully inform the reader's practice and work, the endeavor of crafting this volume will have been worthwhile.

Michael Stepniak
Dean & Professor of Music
Shenandoah Conservatory of Shenandoah University

1 Changing the Game for Music in Higher Education

David Cutler

Change.
Perhaps the most challenging word in the English language. Also, among the most necessary.

Never has this been truer than today, at least for those hoping to thrive during this era of intense societal transformation and exponential disruption. Though there is no generic, replicable success formula, one path guarantees failure: stagnation. What got you *here* certainly won't get you *there*.

Time and again, the 21st century has punished organizations and industries that fail to adapt to a radically evolving world. Consider the plight of record labels, newspapers, bookstores, and brick-and-mortar retail. Those hoping to win the game of relevance and sustainability must pursue change with the discipline and commitment of an Olympian (or, better yet, a trained musician).

While change is difficult in any sector, it poses a particular challenge for music in higher education. Music's long, proud tradition is both inspiring and firmly rooted in recreating the past. And universities, despite obvious strengths, famously operate as slow-moving bureaucracies. Any seasoned faculty member will confirm that even minor curricular tweaks or policy revisions can trigger endless red tape.

It would be foolish to think that music schools are somehow exempt from the need for constant innovation. Numerous programs have already been downsized or eliminated. Even the healthiest institutions confront unprecedented hurdles. Given the hand we've been dealt, many have argued we are destined for obsolescence. Do we realistically have a chance to emerge victorious?

I believe we do. Much of my optimism stems from knowledge of a powerful secret weapon: *music faculty*. Few groups are more diligent and committed to excellence. Though this battle may be existential, there is no army I'd rather call my own.

But a positive outcome will not happen without intervention. Vision, strategy, and relentless resolve represent our best chance.

As a multi-genre pianist/composer and the world's first tenured music entrepreneurship professor (University of South Carolina), I am fascinated with the concept of innovation. Leading change processes for countless arts, education, and business organizations—including two industry-wide Carolina/College Music Society Summits on curricular reimagination—has taught me a great deal about what it takes for our intricate ecosystem to embrace bold, new thinking. My hands-on methodology turns creative challenges into team-based "GAMEs," an approach presented in my visual book *The GAME of Innovation* and summarized later in this chapter.

I do not prescribe dogmatic, generic solutions that magically solve our industry's woes. In fact, doing so would be antithetical to my message since innovation requires each community to discover unique solutions. Instead, this writing poses provocative questions and actionable strategies for building an entrepreneurial culture.

> Throughout these pages, I will dare to challenge widely accepted conventional wisdom. My point is never to poke the bear or needlessly attack our system. Rather, it is to explore new realms of possibility. What if we did things differently? Might there be a better way? Innovation demands this kind of assumption questioning.
>
> When beliefs are tested—no matter how gently or persuasively—human nature is to react emotionally, too often shutting down. My ask is that readers seriously consider even the most unexpected of possibilities. In fact, if something rattles your cage, lean in. Though you may or may not ultimately come to agree, open minds must prevail if we are to reimagine our destiny.

If you, like me, believe in music education's profound value, play the game of change as if our future depended upon it.

It very well might.

5 Critical Questions

With an eye towards relevance, impact, and long-term health, here are five critical questions every music program should consider.

1. What Do Students Need?

Which skills and perspectives are most necessary for music students?

During the 20th Century, there was a near consensus: *musical excellence*. Whether that meant performance alone or topics like theory, history, and education, outstanding artistry was the entire game. As pedagogy became evermore effective, student achievement leaped off the charts. We were extraordinarily successful at achieving what we set out to do.

Today, however, that limited assumption rings hollow. Do we also have an obligation to prepare majors for career, financial, and personal success? Should we emphasize topics like entrepreneurship, multiple genres, creative problem-solving, arts advocacy, personal wellness, community engagement, social justice, interdisciplinary collaboration, audience development, written/verbal communication, technological savvy, business skills, and global citizenry?

Few educators argue against the merits of such aptitudes. But how can they conceivably be woven into densely packed degrees, already bursting at the seams with quality content? No amount of innovation can add minutes to a day. *Adding almost certainly requires subtracting.* Such change necessitates serious soul searching, and possibly painful cuts.

Reimagining priorities mandate difficult trade-offs. Every decision comes at the expense of a thousand others. So, which is MORE important? Twelve-tone theory or personal finance? Classic medieval history or contemporary composition by the underrepresented? Arranging a tune or arranging career strategies?

If we are to modify focus, there are questions of placement and faculty expertise. When might such topics be addressed? During lessons, ensembles, core academics, electives, extracurricular programming? Do we even have qualified personnel to lead these efforts?

Implementing changes to address the needs of contemporary learners will not be easy. Yet if we fail to act, can we ethically continue to collect tuition dollars?

2. How Are We Different?

In the 20th Century, one of the most important questions posed by music schools seemed to be: "How does our program look essentially like all others?" Whether big or small, public or private, they loved to boast, "We do ALL the same things as Juilliard/Eastman/other famous conservatories!" (And our orchestra is only 26% worse! Our theory is 2% better!)

As a result, most units embraced near indistinguishable entrance requirements, degree titles, curricular structures, job descriptions, promotion guidelines, ensemble types, recital expectations, and capstone projects. Furthermore, this approach worked. Students came. Programs proliferated. Music schools thrived.

Today, another question may be necessary to flourish, or even survive. "How is our program *different* from all others?"

Meaningful distinction is the new gold standard. Here are a few reasons why:

- **Recruitment.** In a cutthroat, shrinking market, clear differentiation offers a competitive advantage.
- **Student preparation.** Many career paths are oversaturated with talent. Are there distinct ways *your* graduates will excel and stand out from the crowd?
- **Reputation.** "Very good" or "the same but better" are challenging marketing messages in the 21st Century. "Different" is stickier and more easily understood.
- **Revenue.** Digitized coursework will increasingly be created by some organizations (including those outside of academia) and licensed to others. Schools with differentiated content have an opportunity to expand reach and revenue.

Whether differentiation involves values, degrees, or something else, regional/national leaders reap big rewards. What makes you special?

3. Who Do We Serve?

In the past, defining a music school audience was simple: students pursuing performance, composition, and education degrees. (Though Bachelor of Arts majors were also our responsibility, they were often viewed as second-class stepchildren.) Today, for a host of financial, ethical, and aspirational reasons, the water is murkier.

Do music programs have an obligation—and opportunity—to impact learners across campus? What new degrees would increase enrollment? Should we actively engage underserved populations to help thwart systemic poverty and our own histories within systemic racism? Does our programming represent local demographics? Might we become an *arts hub* offering events, education, and edification to "non-traditional" audiences? In fact, can we play a role in economic development, cultural visioning, or community branding?

4. Might We Lead the University?

For music programs to succeed, university-level support is requisite. Natural allies buy into the inherent power of the arts. Proactive communication may be all it takes to earn their unflappable support. But even skeptics not yet on the arts bandwagon can be swayed. When music proactively embraces institutional priorities, goodwill follows.

For example, universities often claim to embrace values like EDI (equity, diversity, and inclusion), community engagement, service-learning, leadership, and interdisciplinary collaboration. Yet substantiation can be illusive. Music programs that step up as early adopters and eager partners experience a number of wins beyond embracing the value itself: student/faculty/community impact, enhanced reputation, media attention, fresh funding, administrative/board support, etc.

In what ways might your program be the first, show the way, and lead the charge?

> At the University of South Carolina, "entrepreneurship" has long been a stated institutional priority. Interestingly, the School of Music was the first USC program to introduce a minor in this topic. We were also the first music school anywhere to introduce an entrepreneurship minor.
>
> This didn't happen magically. It required leadership and a community willing to do the hard work of change. As a result, university leadership, business faculty, and other colleagues often point to music as a model for the rest of campus. This kind of exciting positioning benefits even non-related goals.

5. How Can We Remain Sustainable?

In order to offer robust value to the world, our doors must be open for business. But let's face the obvious: music schools are expensive. Particularly costly features include:

- **Private lessons.** Typically, the only one-on-one instruction across campus.
- **Small class sizes.** Music programs rarely offer mega-courses with 100+ students.
- **Large ensembles.** Though groups maintain rosters of 50+, they also famously claim just 1-credit per student, despite meeting multiple hours per week (typically 3 – 6). Sometimes 0-credit participation is permitted, further reducing profitability.

- **Resources.** Instruments, concert halls, keyboard labs, and practice rooms require significant investment.

Historically, universities have subsidized poorer programs with the profits of others. But that is increasingly frowned upon, even forbidden. As state funding shrinks, fewer applicants pursue music degrees. New business models compete with traditional university education. Administrations scrutinize budgets with exactitude. Units are required to pony up and amplify profitability. Less lucrative areas are slashed. The bottom line determines fate.

In many cases, the percentage of state dollars shrinks within public institutions' budgets. Supply-and-demand ramps up as the number of high school graduates entering college falls off a cliff, and new educational models compete with traditional university education administrators to scrutinize budgets...

Given this reality, how can we ensure durable viability?

> Fortunately, there are plenty of ways music schools can improve financial standing:
>
> 1 Introduce new degrees/programs that secure additional music students.
> 2 Attract more students to existing music degrees/programs.
> 3 Expand classes that engage students across disciplines.
> 4 License digital content to reach expanded audiences.
> 5 Increase philanthropic/corporate giving by making music's value proposition explicit.
> 6 Secure more/larger grants.
> 7 Form partnerships with private industry that generate profits for both.
> 8 Reduce expenses through efficiencies or cuts.
> 9 Secure supplemental university funding by championing campus-wide initiatives.
> 10 Invent/increase other sources of revenue (ticket sales, summer programs, merch, etc.).

Overcoming Systemic Obstacles

I often hear progressive colleagues bemoan that music faculty are stuck in the past, ardently opposed to anything remotely forward-leaning. As evidence, they cite areas like curricula that have barely budged in decades, despairing "It's a *conservatory,* after all, not a *progressatory.*"

Though I feel their pain, this has rarely been my experience. The diagnosis feels off.

True, some faculty are dead set against evolution. They teach only as they were taught. The future must mirror the past. End of story.

But these are rare exceptions. Most music faculty are reasonable, engaged, and open. They care about relevance and are willing to consider alternatives.

When leading change processes for music in higher education, I typically find a sizable population eager to roll up their sleeves and dream. They are quick to laud proposals...that *others* might pursue. "Let's add new classes!" (...to be taught by fresh hires...) "Let's advertise more aggressively!" (...just don't touch my area's budget...) As long as modifications steer clear of personal responsibilities or resources, these professionals flash the green light for evolution.

A second group goes further as if to argue, "I am the change! I've already changed!" Perhaps they adopted a textbook, flipped the classroom, and programmed contemporary music. During Covid-19, a significant leap included virtual teaching.

These may well be positive developments. Such surface tweaks, however, are unlikely to produce the dramatic, systemic overhaul needed to meet the moment.

Which brings us full circle. Understandably, institutional paralysis frustrates those committed to bold innovation. But don't blame obstinance. *Our people are not the problem.* In fact, they are our brightest lights. Rather, turn attention to systemic obstacles that handcuff progress.

Fortunately, there are keys for unlocking these shackles.

Lack of Training

Music faculty wholeheartedly embrace the value of training. Many of us started artistic journeying in diapers. Countless hours have been devoted to private lessons, practice, and improvement. As a result, we've got chops.

Training is more than our job. We are education advocates. To cultivate skills or expertise—be it instrumental performance, theory, written communication, neuroscience, whatever—we know the secret: Find an instructor, take a class, read literature, "shed." To develop fluency with just about anything, get yourself trained.

But does this philosophy extend to creative problem-solving? One common innovation myth is that you either have it or you don't. Some fortuitous prodigies were bestowed with magical gifts at birth. Sadly, the rest of us are predestined to impotent normalcy. Imagination just isn't "our thing." (Similar assumptions are widespread about improvisation.)

Others presume creative propensity is inherent, readily available to anyone with an open mind. *To innovate, simply jump in!* Considering this (false) perspective, it is understandable why proponents come to believe that those who resist are scared, stubborn, and recalcitrant.

In reality, neither is true. While some people have more natural ability, innovation (like music) is a skill to be cultivated. Excellence requires technique, strategy, training, and practice.

Yet few universities offer electives in design thinking, let alone require them. Creative problem-solving is bypassed during lecture-based, fact-focused curricula. Most adults don't work for companies like IDEO Labs or Apple, where continuous reimagination is habitual. In fact, they have never witnessed truly innovative environments from the sidelines, let alone participated in one.

Music faculty (particularly those with classical backgrounds) have been shaped by a worldview that reveres *authentic performance practice*. A performer's "job" is to play the "right" notes, rhythms, articulations, and dynamics as prescribed by a composer in stylistically informed ways. If there is room for creativity, it is limited to minor surface tinkering (adding a crescendo, changing the fingering, adjusting the music stand). While the classical tradition offers glorious benefits, disciples are not taught the art and science of innovation. In truth, years of cognitive programming have conditioned them to "not innovate."

Given these realities, it is no mystery why music faculty struggle with change. Without training or exposure, how can we reasonably expect them to excel? To improve odds, we must invest time and resources in (re)training our people.

Instrument-Think

Innovation rarely requires inventing the proverbial wheel from scratch. Most often, it results when distinctly different worldviews intersect. An idea from one place is applied elsewhere.

In theory, universities should be breeding grounds for experimentation. The close proximity of so many smart people spanning vast disciplines is perhaps academia's biggest asset. Yet interdisciplinary exploration can be in short supply. Colleagues often don't know what happens across the hallway, let alone down the road. Silos are ubiquitous.

Though music programs draw from narrower perspectives than the breadth of a university writ large, diverse thought is nonetheless

present. Each area is shaped by distinct worldviews and traditions. Unfortunately, even that potential gets squandered when programs architect narrow, ultra-specialized sub-silos.
I call it instrument-think.
Instrument-think runs rampant across music programs. The larger the unit, the more pronounced the symptoms. It is evidenced in the creation of "divisions" and "departments" (isolating words in themselves), juries, recital committees, search committees, chamber groups, extracurricular offerings, and more. As a result, self-confirming biases, untested assumptions, and "conventional wisdom" are continually reinforced.

> A simple example to make the point: At one school I visited, the woodwind area requires students to speak from the stage during recitals. These teachers believe communication skills and audience rapport-building are essential. In the same program, string faculty strictly prohibit any performer to talk during events.
>
> I doubt we live in a world demanding that clarinetists—but not violinists—be verbally articulate. Either this aptitude is important, or it is not. Cross-pollinating might prompt debate on educational merits, audience experience, etc. If an argument resonates, someone's mind might even be changed. Growth is likely.

To open up the culture, actively disrupt the brutal segregation of instrument-think. Build teams and spaces with intention, ensuring ample opportunity for wonderfully diverse worlds to collide. We have so much to learn from one another. Better yet, doing so amplifies community and unified purpose.

Misaligned Incentives

As a rule, students come to value what teachers tell them is important. They adopt priorities of the system in which they are nurtured, whether that entails grades, artistic excellence, creative exploration, social justice, or something else.

Faculty are no different. Professional attention closely mirrors an employer's success metrics. Unfortunately, evaluation rubrics regularly misalign with stated institutional priorities. This makes things confusing for employees and the brand at large. For example, consider frequent inconsistencies between articulated universities' values and Tenure and Promotion (T & P) guidelines (typically 40% teaching, 40% research, 20% service).

- **Entrepreneurialism.** Though many universities claim to value entrepreneurship, even highly successful faculty enterprises may not fulfill T & P requirements.
- **Impact.** While universities reward "high impact" research, what does that mean? Publishing a peer-reviewed article in an academic journal is revered, including esoteric statements read by a few. Contrastingly, viral videos, blogs, or podcasts that break the Internet might not be acceptable citations.
- **Community Engagement.** Many universities outwardly trumpet community engagement. With T & P, however, local efforts are often deemed the less weighted "service," even when positively affecting thousands. A conference presentation in a sparsely populated Bangkok ballroom, on the other hand, constitutes an "international impact" scholarship.
- **Innovation.** Though "innovation" is a top goal for many universities, faculty are not benchmarked on their participation in fostering positive change, never mind being celebrated after a bold failure. In fact, risk-taking change agents may find themselves in peril, while naysayers who maintain the status quo (or even aggressively oppose change) sail through.

> For many academics, T & P is a particularly emotional topic. Highly invested in protecting the historical system in place, they are firmly opposed to even gently questioning its core biases.
>
> Please understand, that I am a tenured full professor and grateful for the designation. My point is not to attack or defend this practice. Rather, when T & P does play a role, might there be ways to better align demands with institutional values and needs? Designed accordingly, T & P can become an important catalyst for promoting dynamic, cutting-edge priorities.

Tenure is offered as an example because it plays such a prominent role in many universities. A range of additional mechanisms inspires faculty action. What framing might help these intrinsic/extrinsic motivators become allies for meaningful change?

- Annual reviews
- Authority
- Awards
- Being part of a team/something meaningful/something bigger

- Bonuses/raises
- Peer evaluations
- Personal goals
- Productivity
- Professional development
- Project support/grants
- Public pats on the back
- Reputation
- Sabbaticals
- Sense of purpose/mission
- Student interactions
- Special assignments
- Teaching assignments
- Travel opportunities

Incentivize what is most important through systems already in place. Metrics matter.

> I am an advocate of "opt-in" over "force-in" or "hobble-out." Celebrate rather than punish.
>
> For example, suppose your community hopes to amplify a value like technological exploration, community engagement, or interdisciplinary collaboration. Rather than requiring all faculty to participate or shunning those who don't, reward colleagues who do. Publicly celebrate early adopters, and warmly invite participation. To foster growth and risk-taking, carrots are more effective than sticks.

Upside-Down Faculty Priorities

Music faculty are resoundingly dedicated employees committed to doing their job—the position outlined in their contract—with care and excellence. In fact, professors often go further. They become fierce "discipline defenders," taking extraordinary measures to develop and protect their island. (The devoted tuba teacher must advocate all things low brass. That's the gig!)

The care these professionals bring is admirable. But such a mindset can foster silos and protectionism. It pits colleagues against one another, who are forced to compete for finite resources in a zero-sum game. Change in the name of institutional priorities (including even sustainability) is met with suspicion or resistance, particularly if visioning threatens "what I was hired to do."

Belief systems valuing discipline-demands-first, employer-needs-last are upside down. Despite good intentions, they undermine long-term success.

School-wide innovation requires a paradigm shift. Since everybody plays a vital role in shaping students, culture, and success, how might we create environments where employees instead view themselves as interlocking puzzle pieces?

Imagine if the highest honors were bestowed upon stakeholders who try something new, shuffle the deck, elevate the performance of those around, or even give up discipline-specific resources in the name of positive change.

Bottom-Up/Top-Down Leadership

Thanks largely to the oversight required of their positions, music executives (deans, directors, etc.) are likely to have a comprehensive view of program intricacies. Supervising multiple units places them in regular contact with various interest groups. Upper administration interactions illuminate national trends, institutional goals, external threats, and ripe opportunities.

But when it comes to the game of change, some executives shy away from any but the smallest, incremental tweaks. Despite pressing needs, bold action feels too scary, too risky. Justifying this hands-off approach, I've heard many concede that change (regrettably) does not fall under their purview. Common rationalizations include, "curriculum is the sole domain of faculty," "with our measly budget, we lack the resources to change," or "unfortunately, my hands are tied."

Of course, faculty without guidance do not believe they are responsible for leading change (argued in the previous section). Therefore, programs with hands-off administrators get stuck.

One explanation for this apprehension stems from a structural peculiarity. In the corporate world, leaders are evaluated primarily/solely by their boss. When navigating turbulent times, they may be given a directive to do whatever it takes to achieve long-term success.

In contrast, higher education deans are evaluated by more than their supervisors. Faculty also vote on retention. Despite obvious benefits, this accountability can foster deep-seated fear of making waves. No matter how valuable or necessary progress may be, the act of change is always difficult. Threatening the comfort of familiarity, it may ruffle feathers and prompt negative reviews. Rather than taking that chance, many executives remain passive.

Another type of leader has courage and ambition. Armed with revolutionary ideas, they single-handedly reimagine frameworks and enforce proposals. Nothing can stop their commitment to what is right and necessary. *It's my way or the highway.*

Progressive outsiders may applaud such visioning. But in all likelihood, this approach is doomed to implode. For starters, one person is unlikely to have all the best insights. Furthermore, faculty do not appreciate hierarchically forced evolution. Dogmatic mandates fly in the face of academic freedom. Regardless of intent, the likeliest outcome is rebellion, even outright mutiny. Morale plummets. Folks dig in their heels. The leader may get fired.

Failing to guide the process...Telling people what to do.... Bottom-up and top-down leadership are unlikely to end well.

So, what's the best way to effectively catalyze change?

Great leaders understand the importance of setting the narrative. They determine which issues get highlighted, and in what order. Without prescribing solutions, successful executives are known for designing/facilitating problem-solving *processes* around clearly defined challenges.

But come time to dive in, the community is empowered to imagine a powerhouse future.

To amplify innovation, solve the culture first. Using your bully pulpit, create an environment valuing collaboration, long-term visioning, and shared purpose.

- Invest in innovation training.
- Install silo-busting structures.
- Incentivize organizational priorities.
- Instill workforce values balancing institutional needs with discipline demands.
- Implement well-designed change processes that give power to the people.

"Innovation GAME" Design

When many organizations confront pressing challenges, a single question is deployed. After describing the conundrum, they ask "What should we do?" I fondly refer to this phenomenon as a *one-stop flop.*

Efforts are doomed before they begin. Conversation bounces from topic to topic. Dissent prohibits progress. Time runs away. So much gets said, yet so little is accomplished.

Communities serious about change need to do better. Well before any proposal is hatched, serious leaders design coherent processes. They determine what questions will be asked, in which order, and for how long. While specific solutions are never prescribed, the experience is constructed in such a way that positive outcomes are almost guaranteed.

I call it a GAME.

Any carefully architected process may be considered a game, whether or not it is particularly "game-y." That said, unapologetic gamification offers many advantages. Communities unify behind collective aspirations. Participants become more creative during play than in "real life." Teams are accountable to rules and results. Savvy strategy is compulsory. Multi-team tournaments promote ambition. And though the problem at hand may be exceedingly serious, games bring fun and enjoyment while building camaraderie.

The term GAME suggests a flexible structure.

Guidelines	How is the framework defined?
Arena	Who plays, how long, and where?
Materials	Which tools are incorporated?
Experience	How is the process structured?

What follows is a brief introduction to innovation GAME design.[1]

Determine the Guidelines

Problem management is a puzzle in itself. Which issue should you tackle first? The easy, the low-hanging fruit, the meaningful, the income-producing? Identifying a great challenge is the first test.

Begin by defining the framework for your GAME. *Guidelines* include three parameters:

Challenge	What's the problem?
Constraints	What are the non-negotiables?
Criteria	What constitutes success?

A *Challenge*—the central problem you hope to solve—is summed up in a single, concise sentence. Whether written as a statement or question, its meaning should be immediately clear.

- Reimagine our music education degree.
- Design a powerhouse initiative that serves our community.

- How might we increase enrollment by 25%?
- If juries were eliminated, what would we do instead?

Sometimes, it makes sense to approach two problems in tandem, typically marrying aspirational and logistical issues.

- How might we recruit more students (aspiration) while spending less money (logistics)?
- Improve student outcomes (aspiration) while requiring less time from faculty (logistics).

Constraints are non-negotiable conditions that MUST be incorporated into your solution. Bulleted lists of 2 – 5 entries are typical, once again using succinct, easy-to-understand language.

- Must be implementable within 6 months.
- Cannot cost more than $100,000.
- Happens in Recital Hall from 5 – 7 PM.
- Undergraduate music students from all majors must be included.

> I sometimes hear problem-solvers argue against the need for constraints. "Why don't we rip off the shackles and let imaginations flow freely?" While I appreciate the sentiment, their request is misguided. With infinite possibility and zero limiters, efforts are left without any structure to build around or push against. One of two outcomes is likely: paralysis or the obvious.
>
> Not only are well-designed constraints necessary, but they can also be instrumental in unlocking new and unprecedented thinking.

Criteria implies success. What will the best proposals accomplish? Like constraints, they are also stated as bullet points. Push your team to think big with ambitious aspirations.

"Shortlists" with 2 – 5 entries are most common, though "long lists" including 10+ entries are also possible. In both cases, teams attempt to realize as many points as possible.

- Recruit 20 students. *(Note: as criteria, this is a goal rather than a requirement.)*
- Applicable to transfers. *(Once again, ideal but not requisite.)*
- Win a national award. *(This kind of aspiration encourages big thinking.)*

16 *David Cutler*

A full set of guidelines—Challenge, Constraints, and Criteria—should be presented at the beginning of each GAME and readily visible throughout. An example follows.

The Great Curricular Challenge

GUIDELINES

CHALLENGE:
Design an innovative undergraduate music degree that emphasizes a distinct departmental value.

CONSTRAINTS:
- 120-credit hours maximum.
- May not require more than one new faculty hire.
- Implementable within one academic year.

CRITERIA:
- Highly differentiated from any degree on the planet.
- Attracts twelve students in year 1.
- Integrates multiple musical genres.
- Somehow involves the local community.

Establish the Arena

An Arena describes what you have to work with, and the conditions of play.

Puzzlers   Who forms your problem-solving community?
Period   How long will you have to solve the challenge?
Place   Where does the GAME take place?

Three questions must be considered when determining which *Puzzlers* should play your GAME.

1 **How many teams?** Innovation GAMEs can involve one or multiple teams. A single group offers consistency to all participants. Multiple units develop contrasting solutions, which either compete for adoption or are fused together. Obviously, more entities complicate logistics.

While most of my GAMEs involve 1 – 8 teams, I've run experiences with as many as 12—quite a lot to coordinate!

Changing the Game for Music in Higher Education 17

2 **How many per team?** Typically, 2 – 10 people. More is unwieldy. With each new voice, additional perspectives and brainpower emerge. On the flip side, larger groups diminish individual podium time, and uneven participation becomes likely.
3 **Who are these people?** Will you involve your full faculty, a single unit, or chairs from across the school? Does it make sense to expand the community and invite additional profiles, perhaps faculty from other disciplines, staff, students, parents, or community members? Before sending invitations, carefully consider which backgrounds will be most beneficial. Also, keep in mind that merely participating in a well-run GAME can build buy-in.

> While a full chapter of this book considers issues around diversity, allow me to briefly broach the topic. When building problem-solving communities, I work overtime to engage a diverse mosaic of puzzlers: different ages, races, religions, disciplines, regions, positions, etc. Though there are a number of rationales for such an approach, I do this largely in the name of innovation. BIG ideas are exponentially more likely to emerge when contrasting worldviews intersect.

To determine your GAME's *Period,* balance two competing concerns.

1 How much time is required to solve this puzzle?
2 How much time are your puzzlers willing to devote?

It is possible to play a simple GAME during the span of a typical hour-long faculty meeting. Addressing nuanced content, burrowing into details, and crafting thoughtful proposals require more. Half-day, full-day, and multi-day retreats offer time to explore, invent, and bond. Another possibility involves intermittent sessions, combining a series of experiences (e.g., six 90-minute sessions on consecutive Tuesdays).

Finally, consider where problem-solving will occur. This *Place* can be familiar, like a boardroom, large rehearsal space, or concert hall. Another possibility is using fresh venues such as an open warehouse or hotel ballroom. Foreign environments can add gravitas to the event.

When deciding where to meet, determine the conditions necessary to optimize the experience. Specifically, groups need ample real estate for collaboration. When everyone meets in a single room, each team "owns" a table. For longer GAMEs, it often makes sense to assign separate rooms.

During COVID-19, academic communities increased comfort by utilizing video conferencing. If scheduling a GAME online, design activities that take advantage of your platform's assets (e.g., breakout rooms, typed chat, recording the action), while diminishing its deficits (distributing physical materials, spontaneous side conversations, etc.).

Guidelines and Arena are interdependent. If you have a specific challenge that must be solved, determine ideal conditions of play. (e.g., How long will it take to revise our faculty handbook, and who needs to participate?) If, on the other hand, you start with Arena (we know our faculty retreat involves 50 employees, spans 6 hours, and is scheduled in the Band Hall), design reasonable Guidelines that allow tangible progress to be made given the hand you've been dealt.

Select the Materials

Tools matter. They directly impact what can be built, and how we think. Which problem-solving *Materials* will you employ?

Gatherables Core problem-solving items
Gear   Specialty game components
Gamebords   Mapping canvases

Common problem-solving *Gatherables* include:

- Small paper (post-it notes, index cards, etc.)
- Large surfaces (whiteboards, flip charts, poster board, butcher paper)
- Writing implements (ballpoint pens, markers, Sharpies, crayons)
- Adhesives (tapes, glues, stickers)
- Prototyping supplies (art supplies, toys, anything you can find)
- Technology (laptops, projectors, speakers)

> An important part of any problem-solving process involves note-taking or *scribing*. For many activities, including brainstorming and analysis, effective scribes distill ideas to their essence (1 – 5 words per concept is usually plenty). Capturing concepts concisely allows for fast-paced action and makes ideas easier to locate, discuss, and organize.
>
> There is often a learning curve, particularly for academics accustomed to writing lengthy, complete sentences. Brevity requires practice and technique.

Specialty *Gear* includes items like posters, worksheets, and "concept cards" specifically designed for your GAME. It can also mean dice, poker chips, spinners, roulette wheels, timers, buzzers, and prizes. While not required, these elements add to the enjoyable sense of gaming. When employed strategically, they ignite the imagination in fresh ways.

Some GAMEs include *Gameboards*, where teams map interrelated elements onto a single page. Drawn on flip charts or printed as large posters, they include a variety of fields representing critical aspects. During play, the gameboard is populated with post-it notes. Doing so helps both problem-solvers and observers concisely define/comprehend/analyze/evaluate even complex proposals.

Simple Gameboards include familiar tools like SWOT diagrams and the urgent-important time management matrix (Stephen Covey, *The 7 Habits of Highly Successful People*: New York; Simon & Schuster, 1989). Below is a more sophisticated example, designed for the Carolina/College Music Society Summit 2.0. During various parts of the three-day GAME, diverse teams we required to:

1 Identify two **distinct values** for a hypothetical degree program
2 Define each value with three **descriptors**
3 Propose curricular **activities** emphasizing one or both values
4 Clarify which **course** will incorporate each activity
5 Determine **adjustments** to make room for activities without increasing contact hours

Build the Experience

What happens during your innovation GAME? Which activities, in what order, for how long?

While each GAME is different, they typically require teams to develop tangible proposals that solve the stated Challenge in spectacular ways.

The majority of play involves *Team Time,* where groups are tasked with addressing specific questions or tasks. For example:

- How do we currently approach _____?
- Interview students
- Which resources might we access?
- What if we didn't require recitals?
- Brainstorm concepts
- Develop the details
- Which concept do you choose?
- Offer constructive feedback

Figure 1.1 Curriculum Gameboard from Carolina/College Music Society Summit 2.0

- Map the vision
- Prepare a pitch

Define how each activity will work, considering:

- **Explanation.** How long is needed to introduce the prompt?
- **Materials.** What tools are integrated, and how will they be used? (e.g., write thoughts with pens on post-its, one idea per sheet)
- **Roles.** Does everyone on the team function the same way, or do they assume roles? (e.g., one person interviews, one person scribes, two people listen)
- **Extras.** Are outside people involved with the activity? (Interviewee, consultant, etc.)

Time management is crucial. Allocate intervals so that work can be reasonably achieved. That said, tight deadlines force focus. In fact, quick-paced GAMEs teach puzzlers to become efficient, stop rambling, and get out of the weeds—invaluable life lessons. Things invariably take longer than planned. Don't forget to allocate minutes for an explanation. Always leave buffers, ensuring you don't run out of time before deliverables are complete. A typical schedule might look like:

75-Minute GAME

Introduction	5 minutes	
Activity A	8 min	(=3 min explain, 5 min Team Time)
Activity B	5 min	
Activity C	12 min	
Activity D	7 min	
Activity E	15 min	
Presentations	8 min	
Reflection	10 min	
Total	**70 min**	
(Buffer)	(5 min)	

Designing innovation GAMEs, like building a syllabus or composing a piece, requires technique, imagination, and patience. That said, the investment is worthwhile when a community emerges victorious, armed with innovative solutions, and energized about the future.

> Planning an innovation experience typically takes me at least 3 to 5 times the length of the event, often more.

Sample Activities

Literally, hundreds of activities may be included in innovation GAMEs. Here are a few examples to ignite your imagination.

Assumption Stomping

Without assumptions, life would be impossible.

Yet widely held, untested beliefs often cause individuals and organizations to miss huge potential. Unfortunately, the most deeply held convictions may not even be recognized as assumptions. They're just *the way things are.*

Case in point…I've asked many musical communities: "What's the most important feature music students seek in a teacher?" Typical responses include "a record of student success," "compatible personalities," and "impressive credentials."

These are indeed worthy considerations. But something else takes precedence, I insist. Without fail, the stumped audience challenges me to produce evidence. "The number one priority for music students is finding a teacher who plays *exactly* the same instrument they do. Failing to check that box means automatic disqualification."

You can see a look of embarrassment for this oversight. "Well, of course! That's so obvious, we didn't think to bring it up!" But without recognizing an assumption, how can it be evaluated? Are we certain that mentors specializing in the same thing are always the best solution? Do they provide 100% of what students need, while non-instrument-sharing experts offer zero? What opportunities might we be missing?

A host of hypotheses inform the current design of music schools, including:

- Reading music is essential.
- So are juries.

- Applied study = one-on-one instruction.
- Score instrumentation is to be preserved.
- All music students must receive training in classical history and theory.
- Violin recitals should include a Bach suite, classical Sonata, and Romantic work.
- All faculty members should have their own office.

The problem with conventional wisdom is rarely that it's completely wrong, and the opposite is true. But it usually isn't wholly correct either. Examining assumptions can lead to an exciting discovery. What opportunity lies on the other side of this "wisdom"?

Assumption Stomping challenges teams to think in new ways.

Step 1 *Identify widely held assumptions.*
Step 2 *If we didn't hold those views, what fortune might be unlocked?*

Obstacle Embrace

Assumptions aren't the only innovation opportunity. Consider obstacles.

For obvious reasons, bumps in the road trigger frustration and diminished success. Yet most hurdles carry a silver lining. Better yet, they can lead to superior problem-solving. Adversity is among the likeliest catalysts for change.

For example, suppose an upcoming concert has been long scheduled in your school's Recital Hall. Unfortunately, 2 days prior, the HVAC crashes. No hall activity is permitted for a week. What to do?

An obvious option is canceling the show.

But might there be a better way? With little time to pivot, even unorthodox solutions must be considered. Perhaps, you discover a sold-out real estate conference the same day. Calling the organizer, you ask if your group might perform (for free!) during dinner. They agree. Surprisingly, the audience is larger and more receptive than any you've had in years. It turns out, that this option was a cut above the original. Thank you, stumbling block!

Covid-19 posed major headaches for music higher ed, disrupting every aspect of our model. Did good come out of it? Many educators point to our embrace of video conferencing platforms like Zoom. It took an international pandemic to nudge academia towards readily available technology!

At USC, we were determined to go further. Wondering how musicians might be most valuable during this crisis led us to imagine *Celebrating Local Heroes*. Identifying a diverse mosaic of 10 neighborhood "heroes" representing industries that stepped up during the pandemic (nurses, teachers, EMTs, truck drivers, custodians, etc.), we designed an unprecedented project that touched almost every area of our school. It involved three aspects:

1. **Vignette videos.** Hero interviews, reduced to 3-minute videos, were scored by student composers and recorded by student ensembles.
2. **Community concerts.** Ten events aboard *The Concert Truck* scheduled at meaningful outdoor locations honored each profession. Student groups performed music inspired by their protagonist. A final university show united all ten heroes for the first time to experience faculty chamber music, concert choir, and our university president.
3. **Community Conversation.** This facilitated discussion offered a rare glimpse into the experiences, frustrations, and desires of diverse neighborhood heroes. Musical engagement was integrated throughout, concluding with participants singing in unison. Inspiring to all!

Let no crisis go to waste. Problems can be gifts.

Step 1 *Identify a specific, pressing obstacle.*
Step 2 *How might this hurdle lead to even better solutions?*
Step 3 *Design an initiative that includes unprecedented features.*

Resource RETHINK

Change requires a reimagination of resources, be it money, time, facilities, partnerships, or human capital. For example, suppose your program hopes to support a new initiative requiring $100,000. Unfortunately, the budget is already overextended. This tool helps teams RETHINK their model, weighing a number of options.

Step 1 *What new resources do we want?*
Step 2 *How might we RETHINK priorities?* (map onto a gameboard)
Step 3 *Develop a plan.*

Approach	Definition	Example
Reduce	Scale back the request.	Since $100,00 is out of reach, consider how this program might run with just $50k.
Get **Efficient**	Achieve the same, more, or different with fewer resources.	Moving from private to group lessons frees money and faculty loads. (Another example includes teaching a 12-hour sequence in just 11-hours.)
Technologize	Assign previously human tasks to technology.	License digital courses that are cheaper than hiring faculty.
Hand over	Reallocate/redirect resources to a new place.	Dip into budgets of ensembles, music history, and theory to find some money.
Investigate	Research untapped resources.	See if there are grants you've never applied for that intersect with the project.
add **New**	Secure supplemental resources.	Raise new dollars through a major gift.
Keep	Maintain resource allocation but emphasize something new.	Find ways to support the effort without changing current budget allocations.

Distinct Value Generator

When consulting with university communities, I often ask, "Why should a prospective student choose your school over others? What's your most distinct value?" This question turns out to be a tough one. With consideration, common pride points include: "We provide a warm, caring environment!" "Our faculty are outstanding!" "The students get good grades!" All wonderful features, indeed.

But are they *unique selling propositions* (USPs)? Will they help your program stand out? *Distinct Value Generator* helps communities work through the process.

Step 1 *What are the current strengths of our program?*

Brainstorm what you already do well. This might include curriculum, cultural issues, facilities, student life, geographical features, etc. Listing strengths is a positive, feel-good activity.

Step 2 *Rate each entry's uniqueness.*

Assign a score to each line item (1 – 5). Rather than considering excellence, however, indicate the percentage of music programs that would likely claim each value.

Score	Meaning
1	80 – 100% of music programs do this.
2	60 – 79% of music programs do this.
3	40 – 59% of music programs do this.
4	20 – 39% of music programs do this.
5	0 – 19% of music programs do this.

This step is eye-opening. Participants suddenly realize that traditionally touted points only tie to the competition. For example, "Our faculty are outstanding," easily receives a '1'. Music in higher education explodes with talent. (If your faculty isn't already stellar, there's another GAME you need to play...)

On the other hand, historically overlooked features suddenly rise to prominence. One program I worked with awarded "all art forms represented in a single building" a score of 4-out-of-5. With further questioning, I learned that despite the close proximity, each discipline currently operated within fully independent silos. Yet discovering this rare asset planted a seed. One of the attendees asked, "What if all our arts students received interdisciplinary education?"

Step 3 *How might we amplify distinctive features?*

The program began considering intriguing angles that exploited their unique potential. Interdisciplinary arts core. Interdisciplinary arts ensembles. Interdisciplinary arts degrees. Interdisciplinary arts research. Interdisciplinary arts showcases. Doing so provided clues for designing a meaningful, highly differentiated university experience.

How might you become a regional or world leader by doing that which best defines your uniqueness?

Amplification

How might your organization achieve unprecedented success? *Amplification* opens the door. Allow me to share a story.

Most deans receive constant appeals for funding support. Perhaps a faculty member requests $3000 to bring an African ensemble to campus. "This will be amazing for my students! They will learn about culture, art, and community," the excited teacher reveals.

Here's the common response: "I love your enthusiasm. This would indeed be great for students. But as you know, money is tight. That said, I truly want to support you. What could you do if I offered $300?" In other words, how would your dream look if divided by ten? Limited budgets typically mean the pie gets cut into small slices.

One dean employs another approach: "I love your enthusiasm. This would indeed be great for students. But as you know, money is tight. That said, I truly want to support you. What could you do if I offered $30,000?" In other words, how might you amplify the dream tenfold?

Wow!! With that kind of investment, we might schedule an extended residency, start a festival, and send students to Africa for the year! We've gone from a cool one-off to a life-changing transformation.

Of course, discretionary dollars are always limited. Clearly, it is not possible to fund everything, let alone offer regular exponential matching. To amplify impact, the dean supports only a handful of projects, but those that represent truly extraordinary dreaming. As a result, ambitions shoot up. Employees collaboratively design projects of profound significance. The cumulative impact explodes. In the end, her fixed budget makes much more of a difference.

As we age, too many of us start to think smaller. Sure, it would be great to change the world. But for now, under these circumstances, let's just get by...

Those who courageously pursue change often seek incremental solutions. "How might we move the needle by 1%?" That's a problem if bold innovation is in order. With incremental goals, people overwhelmingly employ the same old strategies, only a little better. If you have 141 students but desire 145, the framework pursued likely looks much as it always has.

Big, audacious goals, on the other hand, force new thinking. To get from 141 to 500, radical reimagination is the only hope. Better yet, there can be success in failure. Even if just 362 (or 153) students are ultimately secured, that's far superior to the previous modest goal of 145.

Step 1 *Identify a current or modest outcome.*

Measurable goals (including a number) offer a clear starting point. For example:

- $250,000 = annual fundraising
- 45 = average audience size
- 4000 = social media followers

Step 2 *Pick a substantially higher goal.*
Step 3 *Design strategies for realizing highly amplified results.*

Push yourself to think as never before. Consider even the most unconventional of possibilities. When someone begins by saying, "here's a crazy idea," listen up. Rare treasure may be close.

If an invented solution is truly out of reach, it is usually possible to scale back. And almost any puzzle can be solved with enough commitment and creativity.

Big dreamers—who know how to execute—are like great artists. They have a vision and commitment to getting things done.

9 Additional Tactics

While creative, collaborative problem-solving is essential, it is not enough. Innovative cultures embed values that matter most through all they do. Given academia's unique realities, which initiatives are likely to make a difference? Consider the following affordable, implementable, highly effective tactics.

1. Culture Statement

Every music school has a *mission statement* defining what they do and why. The efficacy of such declarations is an important conversation for another time. But it is a concept with which we are all familiar.

Additionally, I advocate creating a *culture statement*.

One of my favorite examples is "10 Family Core Values" by the online shoe vendor Zappos, whose website claims, "more than just words, they're a way of life." With points like (2) "embrace and drive change," (3) "create fun and a little weirdness," (7) "build a positive team and family spirit," and (8) "do more with less," employees have clear guideposts on what matters most.

I recommend music schools develop *"Team Tenets."* This type of cultural statement turns collaboration into ART.

- Attitudes.   Which beliefs embody our culture?
- Rules.   Which laws govern our meetings? (Do's and Don'ts)
- Traditions.   Which rituals are unique to us?

Attitudes, typically 5 – 10 succinctly stated points, forecast desirable mindsets. Healthy attitudes boost morale and contribute to a desirable work environment. In addition, they become indispensable when guiding teams through change processes.

Here are the Attitudes I apply to my own projects and life.

1　Almost every problem is solvable
2　"We" is greater than "me" (and more FUN!)
3　Embrace diversity through all we do
4　Dreams first, then logistics
5　Amplify curiosity and ambition
6　Especially today, yesterday rarely describes tomorrow
7　Find clues where no one else looks
8　Seize opportunity in roadblocks
9　Insist that positivity rises in parallel with difficulty
10　Consider turning the puzzle over and discarding half the pieces

---

Rules address meeting protocols and making expectations clear and consistent. For example:

Do:	Don't:
• Be punctual	• Chezzck tech
• Be present	• Participate in side conversations
• Be respectful of other viewpoints	• Ramble

Traditions foster team spirit, helping participants feel like more than a collection of individuals. Think fraternity secret handshakes. Perhaps you unify behind a clothing item (purple socks), object (ugly coffee mugs), insider song (unofficial anthem), or celebration spot after each big win (favorite local dive). Distinctive rituals build camaraderie and memories.

While culture statements can be developed by leadership, they are more effective when envisioned collaboratively. Invite your community to define the ideal work environment. Brainstorm, vet concepts, and perfect entries. Once the list is set, have everyone agree to terms. Post these commitments visibly, review them periodically, and build the future accordingly.

Either you shape culture or the culture shapes you.

2. Meetings

Let's be honest. Few people feel a giddy sense of anticipation when hearing the words "faculty meeting." Typical gatherings are characterized by project overviews and policy updates that could easily have been distributed electronically. At best, they feature pertinent lectures followed by Q & A. At worst, they are soul-sucking "brain dumps" with thousand-word PowerPoints of questionable relevance.

There is another way!

Faculty meetings represent the rare occasion where your community—your talent—convenes. What if these sessions were transformed into riveting, anticipated perks of the job? How might they become engaging forums to grow as a team, tackle important challenges, tap into collective genius, and model innovation?

My top suggestion involves:

1 **Play.** Even one hour offers sufficient time for an innovation GAME, working on teams to dream and make tangible progress.

A host of additional frameworks are available. Meetings are excellent times to:

2 **Reflect.** Contemplate where things stand, what is working, and what can be improved.
3 **Provoke.** Pose provocative questions: What if? How might we? What then?
4 **Train.** Introduce/practice innovation/collaboration techniques that help teams work effectively, cultivate creativity, cope with conflict, and develop empathy.
5 **Interview.** Conduct focus groups with students or alumni, investigating aspirations, concerns, and outlooks.
6 **Present.** Invite faculty to share audacious *BIG ideas* (1 – 5 minutes each). Then discuss.
7 **Discuss.** Host Socratic discourse on readings or pertinent issues.
8 **Debate.** Argue competing positions around potential innovations.
9 **Learn.** Workshop artistic or pedagogical skills with interdisciplinary relevance.
10 **Compete.** Have small teams pitch prepared, bold proposals that battle for adoption.

Regardless of content, effective meetings—like teaching—tap into multiple intelligences. Engage various senses through movement, visual stimulation, discussion, solo reflection, improv exercises, and more.

> Though traditional faculty meetings may be necessary at times, it is possible to achieve balance. What if just one gathering per term addressed nuts and bolts management, freeing others to integrate more active engagement? Or perhaps a Team Tenet Rule states that no more than 10-15 minutes per session can incorporate information sharing.

3. Retreats

Culture building takes time. I advocate scheduling employee retreats (half-day, full-day, multi-day) at least once per year. Whether inviting your entire workforce or just a subset, the value of shared, immersive experiences cannot be overstated.

Design an engaging, through-composed experience (such as an innovation GAME), with a distinct beginning, middle, and end. Resist the urge to introduce a hodgepodge of content. Instead, focus on a single problem or theme. To feel the time was well spent, tangible results must be generated.

4. Professional Development

> "Professional development" is essential to music schools. Yet does this activity live up to its name? The term has come to imply traditional acts of scholarship such as giving conference presentations. While sharing expertise is undoubtedly valuable, doing so does not inherently help employees learn new perspectives/skills and "develop."

Incentivizing participation in a wider range of settings leads to fresh outcomes. For example, suppose faculty are encouraged to attend one workshop per year as "students" rather than experts. Events falling squarely *outside* someone's wheelhouse offer enormous growth potential.

Better yet, promote opportunities that intersect with your school's needs and priorities. For example, to bolster innovation, training in design thinking proves transformational.

5. Assessments

Annual reviews, peer teaching evaluations, and tenure and promotion files (discussed previously) are common faculty assessment tools. "Were enough boxes checked? Was excellence achieved?" A little reframing helps these instruments advance additional goals.

For example, perhaps your school aims to amplify interdisciplinary collaboration. Incorporating rubrics around this value underscores its importance. Doing so encourages both reviewer(s) and the person being evaluated to think more carefully about the priority: current role and opportunities for advancement.

Such inclusions must not be punitive. A perfectly acceptable answer might be "N/A" for a given period. Even then, it provides an opportunity to discuss and dream.

6. Book Club

Educators regularly stress the value of lifelong learning. Here is an easy way teams can blossom together. Towards the end of spring, distribute a particular book to all faculty, junior faculty only, or those who request a copy. Explain that this optional reading will be discussed and debated next fall. Even busy professionals can often find time for one book over the summer.

Effective titles address large-scale issues relevant to your future, such as:

- Higher education critiques/trends
- Creativity, innovation, and collaboration skills
- Equity, diversity, and inclusion
- Technology
- Arts culture
- Current events
- Community issues

7. Hiring Practices

Hiring is particularly important for higher education. Because tenure-track faculty regularly stay 20 –40+-years, it is critical to evaluate more than discipline excellence. Seek candidates who embrace change and progress.

Before drafting any job description, debate what your program needs most. Should it resemble an "average," traditional post, or something distinctive? Thanks to an oversaturation of music doctorates, it's a buyer's market. And for the right candidate, unique posts are more desirable.

Search committees, particularly within large programs, traditionally comprise predominantly similar-discipline specialists.

A team charged with hiring a violinist might include a violist, cellist, bass player, and string educator. Yet this presents the ideal time to override instrument-think and silos. As a rule, I recommend no more than a third of a committee come from the same department. Not only does this diversity acquaint candidates with a wider network, but it plants seeds for interdisciplinary thinking down the road.

Interviews typically involve one- to two-day marathons combining teaching demonstrations, research presentations, recitals, masterclasses, meals, faculty meet-and-greets, and administration meetings. There is obvious merit to these endeavors.

An additional high-value activity involves Socratic discussion around important issues. The candidate and a small cadre (search committee or specially selected group, perhaps even a student or two) consider a topic like recruitment, curriculum, community engagement, EDI, upcoming repertoire, technological innovation, etc. This process delivers many benefits:

1. The candidate is challenged to function as a proactive team member.
2. This unusual, meaningful activity differentiates your interview/program from others (particularly helpful when pursuing candidates with multiple offers).
3. Participants/observers can evaluate the collaborative nature of candidates, their openness to change, and ideas for the future.
4. Actionable insights emerge from each conversation.
5. Internal participants are challenged to thoughtfully deliberate important issues.
6. Sense of team and shared purpose likely grow more than with traditional interviews.

8. *Onboarding*

Beginnings are crucial. Just as the opening notes of a concert set expectations for what's to come, the initial weeks and months of a new hire play an outsized role in establishing an employee's priorities, work ethic, and institutional connection.

Music schools are well served by designing meaningful onboarding processes. Consider how new hires might be challenged to think creatively, collaborate uncommonly, and connect to a larger vision. Doing so increases workplace satisfaction while setting the stage for future contributions.

> Though many universities currently offer onboarding programs, they typically focus on policies and procedures: parking, health insurance, tenure guidelines, and accessing emails. While these are important factoids, they rarely inspire, let alone cultivate entrepreneurial thinking.

My top suggestion involves placing new hires on teams charged with solving important school-wide challenges. Let them know their voice matters from the start. Doing so builds relationships, while solidly anchoring new community members. It also emphasizes the need to proactively advance institutional priorities.

Another worthwhile measure involves mentors. Assign a senior colleague (representing a different discipline) to aid the transition, answer questions, and shape priorities throughout the first year. A short mentor handbook helps ensure consistent, positive experiences.

9. *Additional Opportunities*

Opportunities are everywhere. But opportunities only belong to people who take them. As you consider what and how to change, seek potential in everything. Reimagine current frameworks or introduce new ones. Here's an A - Z list of inspiration points.

- Advising
- Blogs/podcasts
- Committee assignments
- Design challenges
- Ensembles
- Faculty gatherings
- Grants
- Hackathons
- Interdisciplinary exploration
- Juries
- Knowledge pools
- Learning opportunities
- Meetings
- Newsletters/school magazines
- Office design
- Performances/recitals
- Quarterly questions
- Research projects
- Social media

- Teaching assignments
- Undergraduate/graduate advising
- Venues
- Work assignments
- Xylophones (because 'X' is always for xylophone)
- Yearly themes
- Zoom/video conferencing

Next Steps

The game of change is both frightening and exciting. I call upon all music faculty and administrators to enlist as proactive agents in the fight for relevance, impact, success, and sustainability. The choices we make at this pivotal moment—individually and communally—will play an outsized role in determining our fate.

Next step...You're up! What's your move?

Note

1 For more information, my visual book **The GAME of Innovation: Level Up Your Team and Play to Win** (New York; McGraw-Hill Professional, 2022) describes this framework in detail.

For Further Reading

On change and creativity:

Berger, Warren, *A More Beautiful Question: The Power of Inquiry to Spark Breakthrough Ideas*. (New York, NY: Bloomsbury, 2016).

Burke, Brian, *Gamify: How Gamification Motivates People to do Extraordinary Things* (New York, NY: Routledge. 2014).

David Cutler, *The GAME of Innovation: Level Up Your Team and Play To Win* (New York: McGraw-Hill, 2022).

John Kotter, *Change: How Organizations Achieve Hard-to-Imagine Results in Uncertain and Volatile Times* (New York: Wiley, 2021).

Kotter, John P.,& Whitehead, Lorne A. *Buy In: Saving Your Good Idea from Getting Shot Down* (Boston, MA: Harvard Business Review Press, 2010).

On higher education:

Anya Kamenetz, *DIY U: Edupunks, and the Coming Transformation of Higher Education* (White River Junction, VT: Chelsea Green Publishing, 2010).

Clayton Christensen and Henry Eyring, *The Innovative University: Changing the DNA of Higher Education from the Inside Out* (New York, NY: Jossey-Bass: 2011).

Jeffrey Buller, *Change Leadership in Higher Education: A Practical Guide to Academic Transformation* (New York, NY: Jossey-Bass, 2014).

Jeffrey Selingo, *College (Un)Bound: The Future of Higher Education and What It Means for Students* (Boston, MA: New Harvest, 2013)

José Antonio Bowen, *Teaching Change: How to Develop Independent Thinkers Using Relationships, Resilience, and Reflection* (Baltimore, MD: Johns Hopkins University Press, 2021).

Mark C. Taylor, *Crisis on Campus: A Bold Plan for Reforming Our Colleges and University* (New York, NY: Knopf, 2010).

Mary Landon Darden, *Entrepreneuring the Future of Higher Education* (New York, NY: Rowman & Littlefield, 2021).

2 Transforming Community and Ourselves through Heart and Mind Work

A Pathway for Embracing Diversity, Inclusion, Equity, Belonging, and Justice

Jasmine D. Parker

Introduction

How might music in higher education embrace diversity, celebrate inclusion, champion equity, and foster spaces that invite a sense of belonging? And what might be possible if we were to begin that work by interrogating our own individual responsibility for creating welcoming classrooms, organizations, and institutional cultures?

Too often, as individuals and as institutions, we fail to ask the critical questions about how lived experiences, perspectives, values, and ideals shape organizational culture. Yet, these perspectives must be purposefully considered if we are to develop inclusive learning communities. Indeed, inclusive classrooms and learning dynamics can only be realized when individuals, leaders, communities, and organizations ask these critical questions.

Interrogating the four principles of diversity, inclusion, equity, and belonging, this chapter focuses on our individual responsibilities for personal growth as champions for equity and how we can develop the scaffolding required for assigning cultural hierarchical value within curricula, programs, and ecosystems.

Next, we examine the ways in which people show-up and participate in spaces with others and as members of a community.

The goal of this chapter is to illuminate the ways in which our educational communities can shape cultures that inspire a sense of belonging and to show that care – in both heart and mind – can serve as the foundation for all inclusion and equity work – and thus justice.

Diversity of the United States and Its College Student Population

The United States is more diverse than ever before. Statistics gleaned from the 2020 Census reveal that people of racially and ethnically diverse backgrounds – often referred to as people of color (POC) – account for 39.9% of the country's population. Although traditional college-aged demographics are anticipated to flatten in 2025,[1] the 18–24-year-old population in recent decades has experienced historical highs, representing 30.6 million people in 2017 – up from 27.3 million in 2000.[2] The confluence of these two factors – a growing Black, Indigenous, and POC population and steady growth among 18–24-year-olds – has resulted in a traditional college-age population that is more diverse – when considering racial, ethnic, gender identity, and language acquisition – than in any other time in United States history. And they are going to college.

Reflective of the country's growing multicultural and ethnic populace, approximately 45% of currently enrolled college-aged students self-identify as persons of color.[3] Yet, the disparity between the racial and ethnic makeup of college students as compared to faculty and administrators persists. In 2001, the percentage of white-identifying full-time faculty members of all ranks was a staggering 80.1%. In 2018, little had changed with 75% of full-time faculty of all ranks in the United States self-identified as white persons.[4] If higher education hopes to have their faculty more accurately reflect the students, communities, and society they serve, significant and systemic transformational change must be pursued.

As higher education administrators grapple with and implement long-term strategies to address issues of cultural exclusion and inequities on campuses within the student experience, and within the workforce, incremental, yet profound individual-level change can occur today. Faculty members of all racial and ethnic backgrounds, specifically white-identified professors, should recognize and embrace their capacity to discern and then practice better methods of supporting students, with vested interest in supporting students of color and students identifying as belonging to other historically under-resourced and underserved communities.

But where do we begin? White-identifying faculty can take concerted efforts to critically examine how they show-up in the classroom and the extent to which power is wielded or shared. And equally, as important, white-identifying faculty should self-examine their personal ideologies regarding race, ethnic identity, socioeconomic status, national origin, language acquisition, ability difference, military status, religious affiliation, gender identity, gender expression, sexual orientation, marital status, age, and other aspects of how they have come to understand the ways in which they see not only themselves but persons who do not seemingly share their background or similar lived experiences.

I recommend engaging in this reflective practice both consciously and ongoingly. Complementing this, white-identifying faculty and leaders must interrogate the ways in which their pedagogical, methodological, and leadership approaches support or harm their diverse student learners.

Conceptual Framework to Embracing DEIB

This chapter is a reflective narrative written in the first-person. And while I am an interdisciplinary social science researcher by training, the methodology underpinning this writing is that of a diversity, equity, inclusion, and belonging (DEIB) leader-scholar-practitioner, with components of care, support, empathy, and love detailed throughout. Thus, this chapter is largely a methodological and pedagogical articulation of how I have been able to successfully engage in the work as a DEIB administrative leader, while leveraging aspects of my teaching and research strengths in support of others.

In this chapter, I draw upon elements and practices of a breadth of disciplines. This approach was purposefully pursued as true, holistic, and sustainable DEIB-forward movement, encompassing aspects of identity development, communication, counseling, life and career coaching, teaching, management, leadership, entrepreneurship, mediation, risk assessment, and conflict resolution, among other skill sets. The utilization of these skills shapes and reinforces the foundation of inclusive community space-building. Inclusive community-space building centers bravery and kindness, as methods of heart and mind work, by first infusing them with the American psychiatrist M. Scott Peck's conceptual framework of "true community," then by in-tandem harnessing courage and justice as love for advanced, inclusive, and equitable environment shifting.

Peck defined a true community as the coming together of "a group of individuals who have learned how to communicate honestly with each other, whose relationships go deeper than their masks of composure, and who have developed some significant commitment to rejoice together, mourn together, and to delight in each other and make the conditions of other's our own."[5] This framework coupled with researcher-storyteller

Brené Brown's four-element definition of bravery – which includes vulnerability, clarity of value, trust, and rising (or the continuous acquisition of new skills) – amplifies my view and practice of inclusive community space-building.[6] The holistic adoption of true community competencies compounded by the elements of bravery establish and frame the conceptual framework of my practice.

These principles, which require ongoing and honest holistic feedback from ourselves and others, make possible the construction of environments in which lived experiences, new information, and (un)learning lessons may be shared and gifted to fellow community members. Such efforts are the practice and approach to radical love. Therefore, one may reason that the competencies required to embody, foster, and sustain inclusive community space-building as an interactive practice engaged in with others can only be made possible by centering justice as the crux and impetus of love so that bravery in true community may take place.

This ideological frame and understanding of justice have largely been influenced by the works of Dr. Martin Luther King, Jr. who noted that, "what is needed is a realization that power without love is reckless and abusive and that love without power is sentimental and anemic. Power at its best is love implementing the demands of justice. Justice at its best is love correcting everything that stands against love."[7]

Bravery and kindness are necessary attributes when establishing a community space while engaged in the continuous practice of radical love for self and others. All such skills are needed when seeking and engaging in justice-oriented work in learning and creative spaces. Thus, highlighted throughout this chapter is the concept of love as truth-telling, as defined by the feminist theorist bell hooks. As hooks posited, "the heart of justice is truth telling, seeing ourselves and the world the way it is rather than the way we want it to be. More than ever before we, as a society, need to renew a commitment to truth telling."[8] We must honor and acknowledge the truth no matter how hard that might be. In those moments, practicing and extending grace and kindness to self, and then to others is fundamental, because truth-telling is non-negotiable.

Resistance to truth-telling and justice as a form of love typically leads to negative implications, including the limitation for true community to be formed and sustained over time. Lack of trust and honesty reduces the extent to which community members may feel connected to their environment and to one another. As a result, the degree to which people feel psychologically, emotionally, and physically safe to express themselves becomes reduced at best and endangered at worst.

As you continue to move through this chapter, my hope is that you will practice grace by willingly imparting kindness and love to yourself – including in moments when you seek self-forgiveness for past thoughts, beliefs, behaviors, and practices. To do this, however, you must first begin your journey from the spaces of truth.

I hope you know that you can and will survive your truth. You can and should critically question the principles and values unconsciously and consciously taught to you over time.

What messages have you heard about yourself and about others who do not share an aspect of your identity?

What do you tell yourself about yourself?

The lived experiences you have endured and learned from are the building blocks that have equipped you to care with an open heart and mind. Regardless of how challenging and how uncomfortable your reflections and self-examinations may be, taking ownership of the totality of the experiences, while anchoring yourself in patience, loving self-talk, and grace will lead you to revolutionary transformation and healing. Allow yourself to embrace new perspectives and considerations.

The practice of truth, honesty, and justice through heart and mind work allows for the open embrace of DEIB and justice in communities committed to progress. I hope you trust yourself to remain open to the process of learning and unlearning by engaging from this space of unbridled bravery. Community transformation, inclusive classroom, and learning dynamics begin with you. Let's now journey together by actively deconstructing a transformative change process, with those efforts firmly grounded in the method of heart and mind work.

Heart and Mind Work as Method

The two-pronged methodological approach of "heart and mind work" mandates the openness of one's heart and mind for authentic conversation, engagement, connection, and learning-opportunity to become actualized. Practiced in tandem, though distinctly different, heart work and mind work are approaches to inclusive community space-building that yield extraordinary outcomes when applied together. The next sections describe each aspect of heart work and mind work and how these methodological strategies support the embrace of DEIB and justice in educational, professional, creative, learning, and community spaces.

Openness of Heart

Openness of the heart requires that all persons independently evaluate the level of care and compassion they are willing to extend to themselves and the depth of compassion and care they are willing to extend to others.[9] This is an essential aspect of heart work, because just as human-beings thrive on community and connection – two dynamics that are anchored by love – one cannot honestly or fully give the gift of compassion to others – regardless of how similar or different someone's perceived or named identity or lived experiences as compared to our own – if they do not first gift compassion and kindness to themselves. It is impossible to give away that which one does not have. Said simply, each person seeking to create a community dynamic built on care and compassion must first engage in critical self-reflection to determine the depth of care and compassion in their own heart, the extent to which they practice care and compassion by affirming kindness and grace to themselves, and how and in what ways they express care and compassion to fellow community members. Practicing vulnerability and courage are essential functions to the embodiment of kindness and compassion.[10]

By acknowledging the well of compassion existing within the innermost part of one's being, and embracing it with courage and the fullness of the self, individuals become better equipped to bravely express their truths, their needs, desires, growth areas and opportunities, and concerns with fellow members of their community.[11] Most importantly, when individuals are tapped into their personal well of compassion, they can more easily support others in their quest to be in-tune with their compassion well. Mutual support and encouragement are bedrocks of community relational health and sustainability. The authenticity of honoring oneself by naming one's own capacity to be vulnerable when expressing care, compassion, and concern is an essential element of not only heart work but also community dialogue and engagement. Taking ownership of and actively practicing self-compassion and compassion for others from a healthy heart space – in ways both great and small – reaffirms the humanity of individuals and groups as a collective.

To be openhearted is to actively practice empathy. In many ways, openheartedness requires that you surrender to the process and unfolding of life by embracing it and the people along your life's journey. Adjusting one's sails to align with the currents of life is a necessary aspect of compassionate living and learning. For the full embrace of empathy and connection to be amplified any and everywhere – including in classroom and learning spaces – living with an open heart requires that the seeker of care and compassion surrender to its affects.

Heart work allows people to synergistically learn from and *with* others in community. Heart work allows us to connect to the people we meet on a deeper emotional level via their lived experiences. Much like the openness of mind, this practice is challenging to engage in but is no less essential to the process of cultivating and sustaining inclusion among individuals and groups of people who find themselves within and seeking community.

Openness of Mind

Openness of the mind requires honesty and concerted effort in the self-examination of one's personal thoughts, beliefs, opinions, values, and guiding principles. More so, mind work is the deliberate decision to slow down one's thinking and reactions in favor of processing and scaffolding the granular layers of thought so that we experience heightened responsiveness. The purpose of this self-accountability practice is to proactively catch oneself in the moment, as biased thinking surfaces in the conscious state of the mind so that we might immediately deconstruct, correct, and idea-dismantle.

To open the mind to a variety of perspectives, lived experiences, values, beliefs, and ideals outside one's own knowledgebase, it is important to remind the self that there are many people, cultures, heritages, traditions, and social categories among the global world community, all of whom are impacted differently by world and life events. No one on earth – neither past nor present – has had the same lived experience as another. Siblings can grow up and grow old together, having lived near one another for the entirety of their lives, and yet their lived experiences and perspectives will vary.

One's identity, access to opportunity, and personal outlook, in combination with the culmination of events experienced, create a variety of viewpoints and beliefs. We all, as human beings, are given the opportunity to experience life through our personal lenses. And the nuanced experiences we have with events, people, and situations are what most influence our innermost thoughts, outlook, and opinion. Teaching oneself to critically question one's thought patterns regarding "the other" allows for the consideration of new perspectives, ideas, and beliefs.

When supporting individuals on their journeys of mind work, I engage them in intensive self-discovery and awareness-rooted exercises, much like the following example. The totality of these questions and prompts permits the answerer to identify the journey they face and the depth to which they aspire to unlearn, so that they may feel and belong in an inclusive community. Lean into your courage and kindness, then take your time as you respond to the following:

- Describe a value or lesson (whether consciously or unconsciously) that your family taught you about race.
- How did your family's values shape or contribute to how you see yourself?
- How did your family's values shape or contribute to how you see "others?" Please note that the use of "others" is deliberately broad so that you may frame your response in the way that best articulates your personal definition of "the other."
- In what ways has your viewpoint shifted, if at all, over time?
- What values or ideals continue to take precedence in your belief system today?
- On a scale of 1–10 (with 1 being not racist at all and 10 being extremely racist), how racist are you?

Reflective thinking is the impetus of information processing. By identifying biases, assumptions, or negative emotions, and analyzing their toxic or mis-truthful origins, one's ability to discern thoughts of (in)equity and (in)justice becomes strengthened.[12] Such exercises diminish barriers to inclusive community space-building practices and environments. This metacognitive approach supports the heart and affective process by providing language for the feelings and emotions one is experiencing. As individuals continue to work on themselves by processing and deconstructing their biases, the process of mind work introduces people to the beauty and fullness of varying cultures and identities. In this way, this exercise allows culturally responsive teaching to thrive because, with the slowing down of our innermost (un)conscious thoughts, followed by questioning their origins and value, we make space for cultural nuance and difference.

Concerted commitment to mind work requires deep learning of the self, which leads to deep cultural awareness. The practice of open mind work also shines light on the impact to which relationships have influenced one's opinions of both self and others. Heart and mind work, when coupled together, allow all who engage in the practice to recognize the deeply rich value of other people, their experiences, and their cultures – even when they have not experienced them firsthand.

Practicing heart and mind work in this way authentically and substantively drives connection to the self, thereby making way for the establishment of and connection to deeper and truer community.

Heart and Mind Work in Action

The saying, "people who live in glass houses shouldn't throw stones" is reflective of the need to first engage in internal or intrapersonal critical self-reflection, self-examination, self-improvement, and growth work before being critical of others. Unfortunately, when this does not happen, people sometimes deflect, discharge internal turmoil or pain, amplify ill-formed perceptions, feelings of unworthiness, biases, or other forms of human-powered injustice onto others. Such actions damage relationships and hinder group culture.

Intrapersonal reflection should be an ongoing self-regulation and inquiry-to-action based process wherein individuals ask critical questions of themselves with self-accountability and course correct, as a result. The questions asked are ones that only the self can honestly answer, as the responses are based on one's own dispositions. A commitment to and active practice of critical self-reflection strengthens the likelihood that heart and mind work will sustain authentic and inclusive community space-building.

I define intrapersonal reflection as the ability to cognitively unpack one's beliefs through the elements of honesty, ownership, trust, love, and capacity-building in ways both kind and challenging. For the fostering of inner harmony, intrapersonal reflection and communication should be practiced using these guiding principles:

- Be honest with yourself so that you may practice honesty with others.
- Own *your* lived experiences.
- Recognize your personal growth areas and continued capacity to (un)learn.
- Reserve the right to change your mind when new insights are discovered or presented.
- Challenge yourself to move through the process.
- Be trustful of yourself. Know that you will not break, despite the degree of discomfort.
- Be loving to yourself by operating from the space of grace.

In further support of heart and mind work, I encourage you to actively engage in continuous self-reflection, as you speak to yourself and to others. The following questions should be asked of the self and are provided as a framework for non-judgmental, yet accountability-driven critical inquiry:

- What is driving this line of thought?
- Where did this opinion, assumption, or belief come from?
- Who taught me to believe this?
- How much influence or impact did the person/group responsible for teaching me this thought have on my life?
- In what ways has this belief benefitted or hindered my ability to show-up as my full self in a community or groups of people?
- How has this thought affected how I perceive other people?
- Have I been exposed to information that may cause me to think differently about this person/group/place/thing?
- If I have not yet been exposed before, then why do I believe this thought to be true?
- What am I willing to do to break the cycle of misinformation; of safeguarding one's perspectives?

Heart and mind work are integral, action-oriented approaches for communal health and collective upliftment. Yet, heart and mind work cannot on their own lead to the fostering of inclusive communities or spaces. Inclusive language and communication, coupled with emotional intelligence (EI) strategies grounded by compassion further strengthen heart and mind work.

Emotional Intelligence Strategies in Heart and Mind Work

Complementing heart and mind work – much of the effort involved in creating a healthy environment in which DEIB may flourish – is dependent upon EI and interpersonal communication dynamics. How people view themselves – the extent to which they identify their growth areas and subsequently take ownership of their lived experiences and related emotions – directly impacts their capacity to empathize and hold space for others. For example, assessing how you see yourself, your life, and your life's journey is core to your self-development. Self-development, specifically how you assign value to your lived experiences and life events, or circumstances actively impacts your ability to embrace the self despite your flaws or imperfections. This is a revolutionary act of self-care and love. Such love becomes magnified when harnessed and used for the intimate processing of circumstances impacting people you may not know well or at all. How you choose to communicate your depth of care, concern, and love of others are all impacted by the depth to which you love yourself. Thus, your capacity for communicating and identifying with those inside and outside of your identity or community group may shine light on the areas of growth and opportunity awaiting you in your practice of heart and mind work. The commitment to the unpacking of such experiences and thoughts keenly impacts community interpersonal communication. This paired with the depth to which individuals are in-tune with their individual and collective emotional well-being drives communal vitality.

Defined by psychologists John D. Mayer, David R. Caruso, and Peter Salovey in 2016, EI is the dual recognition, connection to, and care of one's own emotional state and that of others.[13] For leaders, teachers, and students to feel supported in a learning environment, they must be devoted to deliberately checking-in on their emotional state and earnestly seeking to understand the emotional state, and thus the context, of others. Learning the capacity to which you identify, relate to, and are (de)sensitized by another's lived experience is challenging, yet essential work.

Although some events and lived experiences are easier to understand or relate to, EI in practice heightens the capacity to take-in another's experiences and empathetically feel their emotions regarding the circumstance. EI is a strength that should be leveraged when establishing inclusive community spaces and environments.

The following phrases could be expressed to build connection more deeply with persons seeking community:

- Thank you for sharing your story. That resonated with me deeply.
- Thank you for trusting me with your emotional wellbeing by sharing this aspect of yourself.
- Wow. Your sharing of this lived experience profoundly shifted my viewpoint on the topic. Thank you for being a teacher for me.
- I feel this so deeply *with* you and want you to know that I love and care for you.
- You are worthy.

Compassion and empathy breeds connection. These strengths can be leveraged in times of joy, uplift, and in times of challenge and uncertainty as acts of support in the reinforcement of justice as love.

The following EI-focused questions were written to support you in the interrogation process, as you seek to develop, (re)imagine, and sustain interpersonal community. Given the framing of the questions, it will be important to center and discern the climate and frameworks of your particular communication and engagement concern:

- How did community member(s) verbally react or respond to my contribution?
- How did community member(s) non-verbally react or respond to my contribution?
- Did I pause when speaking to allow others the opportunity to join in verbal conversation?
- How much airtime did I take up?
- What assumptions, if any, did I have going into the conversation?
- In what ways did my assumptions or biases impact how I engaged with others?
- How might my assumptions have skewed my perceptions of community members' energy, approach, and thought regarding the topic or issue?
- What were the driving forces behind why I spoke to the extent I did, and for what reason?
- How much of the engagement was rooted in honoring my ego?
- How could I better support others in community conversation?
- What will I do differently to build a connection with those who find comfort in silently observing the dialogue of others?
- What are the needs of the community?
- Have I asked and listened to feedback with open ears, heart, and mind?

Engaging in ongoing conscious-raising community dialogue and reflection, while actively committing, in both words and deeds, to one's personal growth and evolutionary development enhances interpersonal communication and EI. This practice makes possible substantive and honest, rather than unassuming and wary, conversation. Speaking from the space of truth, engaging in truthful conversation, and wholly hearing the context, content, and subtext of each conversationalist intensifies community spaces.

The establishment and sustaining of inclusive community and learning spaces must involve the entirety of these practices. Such efforts promote intrapersonal reflection as well as compassionate interpersonal and emotionally intelligent discourse between community members.

Here are a few reminders, as you pursue EI and improved interpersonal communication.

- Observe the verbal and non-verbal cues of community group members.
- Hear with your whole body, not simply your ears.
- Be cognizant of the airtime and space you take-up.
- Respond empathetically after processing the information shared by others.

For faculty and administrators, especially those in creative and performance-driven spaces, approaching the profession from the position of empathetic heart and mind work will positively contribute to equity-driven engagement and improved learning dynamics. Heart and mind work creates space for the synergistic exchange of thoughts, feelings, viewpoints, ideas, and innovative creations. Ultimately, this approach enhances student performance outcomes, because the practice allows students to feel and know they are safe while learning, exploring, and creating in a non-threatening or harmful environment. The embrace of heart and mind work thereby supports environments and groups of people as they actively engage in the cultivation of inclusive and equitable spaces. Honoring the value people bring, while amplifying the worthiness of all community members, is made realized in both heart and mind. The invert of heart and mind practices is to be rooted in the ego.

Defeat the Ego

A key element of inclusive and equitable community spaces is the conscious eradication of perceived needs as professed by the ego. The ego, or one's sense of self-worth and value, often becomes the crutch that disallows people from experiencing unbridled support, encouragement, value, and honesty. The ego also reduces the capacity for one to authentically take part in collaboration. These are attributes that, for all intents and purposes, are necessary for community members to feel a sense of wholeness, and for community spaces to flourish.

Often people absorbed by the ego will draw comparisons between themselves and an identity-based community, members of the "in or out-group," or people they find desirable. These comparisons birth feelings of doubt, disconnection, unworthiness, and devaluation internally, and disharmony among groups of people generally – whether knowingly or unknowingly. The ego works against community cultivation, sense of belonging, and collective sustainability.

Unfortunately, teachers, by and large, have not yet realized the extent to which their need to maintain control and dominance in the classroom drives internal conflict and competition. In short, teacher-centered pedagogical and methodological approaches result in a power tug-of-war with the acceleration and need to further feed the ego as a painstaking consequence.[14] The ego calls for people to leverage their internal need for power, insecurity, and external validation by embarking on a quest of dominance over others. This is especially true in traditional teacher-centered learning spaces.

Over the years, I have witnessed numerous teachers' creativity fade or desire to inspire their students/artist-learners dwindle because they became preoccupied in maintaining a teacher-centered disposition, by way of control. Their feelings of disconnect with their craft and with their students most often proved reflective of an internal conflict the faculty members were experiencing. Although they were aware that embracing their students' creative ideas, spotlighting varying student perspectives, extending air space and time, and amplifying the voice and agency of others were fundamental to the function of a participatory, inclusive community, they instead chose to wield power. The truth is these faculty members were undergoing internal warfare and conflict brought on by the ego.

Faculty members in distress are often living in fear of losing the one thing they personally feel compelled to keep tightly bound: power. The journey of creating a healthier and more beneficial living and work dynamic, takes commitment, courage, and relentless pursuit to embody justice as love. This cannot be possible when we are speaking and acting from the ego.

For internal liberation to occur, muting the ego becomes a necessity. This undertaking requires teachers to reconsider their role as lone leaders of a following in favor of embracing a shared commitment and responsibility to become a *member* of their community. What I have learned in my work and through my scholarship is that the biggest barrier to a teacher becoming their best personal and professional selves is their misdirected need to maintain power, control, dominance, and self-centeredness. The reduction and dismantling of this mindset allow good teachers to become masters at their craft and expertly skilled facilitators of said knowledge.

The following tenets are important to remember when actively working to reduce one's ego:

- Be open to the process of growth, whatever that might be and wherever it takes you.
- Embrace vulnerability and not knowing.

- Speak kindly and honestly to yourself.
- Ask yourself what you need and for what purpose you need it.
- Practice hearing and processing rather than listening.
- Remember that acting from the ego is the antithesis of contributing to a sense of belonging and inclusion within a community.

Attributes of Community When Heart and Mind Work Are Practiced

What comes to mind when you hear the word "community?"
What images surface in your thoughts and reflections?
What does your community look like?
Who and what identities of people are present in your community?
Can you name the attributes of the community most essential to you?

These are but a few of the questions individuals and groups must ponder when forming their communal body. Given the variety of responses these broadly written inquiries promote, group members will lovingly learn the multifold needs and priorities of others and themselves.

Below is a brief list that unpacks how we can form communal bodies by approaching relational dynamics from the space of grace and with heart and mind work as its foundation:

- Connection: People long for human connection. Being a part of a community that sees you, that honors who you are, that finds value in your humanity, and that wants to preserve and protect your personhood while supporting your and your group's growth and development are central forces of human connection. Connection gives our life purpose and meaning.
- Honoring of shared values: When group members voice values they find vital in healthy relational dynamics, their descriptions often include their expectations that allow them to personally contribute to the group space. In communities I've witness sustain themselves via shared ownership, members candidly emphasized the importance of trust, privacy, respect for self and others, interdependent accountability, and mutual support as non-negotiable expectations. These terms were agreed upon by each member and with the understanding that members would hold themselves accountable for honoring their shared values. Without a unanimous agreement to the expectations and needs disclosed by group members, communities may face challenges or may even become

unsustainable. To honor shared values means to honor the individual and shared needs of community members.
- Transparency: By operating from the space of grace at both the individual and group level, members become nestled within courageous settings wherein they feel more comfortable expressing themselves, both truthfully and fully. Rather than feel the need to limit or downsize aspects of themselves, community members in inclusive and consciously created environments show-up as their authentic selves because they have the awareness that their community will support them. With transparency also comes the gift of group accountability. Often, group members will pose as peer accountability partners in support of one another's growth and development. Group members practicing transparency and accountability may also call attention to or disrupt commitment violations.[15] Transparency allows for established community vision and values, and the overall collective wellbeing of the group as a priority.
- Willful participation: When community is mutually established, members have a shared sense of ownership and thus become more inclined to participate and engage in dialogue with one another. Additionally, community members become willing devotees to the purpose and values of the group. In this way, community spaces are consciously protected and preserved by its members.
- Relationships: With grace as the premise of community development, group members more willingly express empathy, concern, care, sorrow, joy, and gratitude regarding the circumstances or events impacting their fellow group members. The outcomes of such emotional synergy are the forming of stronger and more authentic relational bonds among and between one another.
- Enriched learning experiences: Candor in the expression of one's needs directly impacts the degree to which individuals and groups of people discern their level of engagement. By engaging in community via graceful, deep, and conscious participation, members maintain a heightened level of openness. Open-mindedness directly impacts the extent to which people express their ability to learn new topics, consider a multitude of perspectives, or contemplate ideologies that differ from their own. The level to which group members have an open mind impacts the likelihood of the community space being an environment grounded in support for trying new things, setting new goals, making new plans, creating new visions, or thinking differently.
- Value: All people have value and *are* valued. These words of affirmation are especially important in inclusive community spaces. The

recognition and wholehearted belief that all people have value goes against what many people have been taught over the years by society. Despite the number of times someone may have heard that they have no value or that they are unwanted, this mindset can be shifted when surrounded and saturated within a supportive, inclusive community.
- Solidarity: The recognition of the humanity and value of fellow community members may cause some members to begin seeing injustices that plague one or few of them as injustices that plague them all. This emotional response to the oppression being inflicted on a single or small group of peer community members also speaks to the depth of empathy embodied at both the individual and group level. Once empathy is heightened in a way that encourages community members to address the commonly felt system of oppression impacting them, the collective moves toward the active practice of solidarity. The work of solidarity demands that all community members recognize how their values, needs, and lives are bound to one another. Embracing inclusive community requires the embrace of solidarity, as one cannot thrive or be sustained without the other. With love-as-justice as the framework for inclusive community space-building, the active embrace of addressing injustices via the amplifying of access to opportunity, inclusive policy, non-discriminatory practices, individual and group mindset shifting, educating others, and speaking out against the systems of oppression that have systemically impacted community dynamics becomes an imperative. Solidarity in heart, mind, and action, breathes life into community spaces.

The make-up of community comprises a multilayer and nuanced blend of attributes, ideals, and people. Community expectations consider the needs and desires of each group member. Actively living one's life gracefully and empathetically, by recognizing that mistakes are merely life lessons with the experiences elevating our capacity to connect and support one another, is the groundwork upon which group dynamics and inclusive community-space building may thrive.

How to Foster Heart and Mind Work as a Pedagogical Approach

Teachers, leaders, staff members, students, musicians, scholars, and other creatives are well suited to develop and embrace inclusive community spaces through the adoption of heart and mind work as pedagogical and methodological approaches. This work, which largely centers the humanization of all people, provides students with the knowledge that they are valued, that their presence adds value to the space and their contributions are welcomed, and that there exists a shared commitment to learn and grow together.[16] In addition to this, heart and mind work when practiced in the classroom or other learning environments foster a sense of shared ownership of the course and learning material, which teachers and students alike will find beneficial.

This grounding is crucial, especially as it relates to the extent to which students feel comfortable candidly sharing how they are feeling about the course and the support they are receiving in the learning experience. This level of belonging enhances the engagement between community members by providing them space and time to impart aspects of their lived histories and identities with one another. Heart and mind work as pedagogical and methodological practices embraces the sharing of a variety of perspectives, while affirming deference.

To effectively facilitate the practice of heart and mind work in the classroom or in positions of institutional organizational leadership, faculty and administrators must be open to examining themselves, particularly how they come into the space before engaging with anyone. Is my mind-state and attitude adversarial or am I exhibiting an inviting disposition? This is a fundamental question to be asked by teachers, leaders, and other persons who are consciously working toward cultivating inclusive and equitably shared spaces. If the answer to this question is the former, then I recommend checking the ego, particularly how the ego is shaping and thus impacting how you see or treat people who you may view to be at or below your status level. Asking oneself to identify and name their energy level as they self-engage or seek to engage others in a communal dynamic is a part of the community cultural grounding and sustaining process. This, again, is fundamental to the embrace of inclusive community spaces.

Often, this frame of questioning will be in some ways unsettling for teachers and students. Why? Teachers do not generally allow themselves or their students time nor space to consider the ways in which they'd like to collectively interact and engage with one another. Instead, the foundational elements of trust are assumed by the teacher, rather than discussed up front *with* their students as a fellow member of the community.

Trust and safety should never be assumed nor taken for granted. In my work, I have witnessed and mediated tumultuous relationships between teachers and students simply because of violated, invisible, unspoken, and thus un-agreed upon expectations. While a professor may assume – and rightly so – that their students will complete their course assignments, one should never assume that their students also wholly and unabashedly trust them with aspects of their intimate identity or lived experience. This is a grave misstep of assumption. Trust must be earned and consented to for the sustaining of an inclusive and welcoming community dynamic.

Asking questions rooted in community development is one of the most important tasks awaiting those facilitating spaces and learning with others. Asking course participants, for example, their vantage point on community allows teachers to better understand how to engage with and honor their students.

Here are some other pedagogically centered questions that help teacher-leaders better learn their students' needs, while establishing and grounding communal spaces. These questions should be asked to all students and community group participants:

- Given your needs, what does "community" mean to you?
- When you see or hear the word "community" what first comes to mind?
- What elements of community are most important to you?
- In this moment in history, how does community feel to you?
- What will it take for us to build a community in which you will feel safe?
- How can we honor ourselves in this space?
- How can we honor each other?
- In what ways can we foster community together?

The practice of heart and mind work in learning spaces relies deeply upon honesty and grace, particularly viewing grace as a gift for the self that should be shared with others. My ideological approach to embodying and practicing grace has been influenced by the work of the American poet and writer Cleo Wade.[17] Wade's iteration of how to embrace others with openness of mind, clarity of heart, and the knowing that a variety of lived experiences – and thus viewpoints and perspectives – exist within heterogeneous community has also shaped my worldview of imperfection.

Community and learning spaces are environments that, when established with heart and mind work as its foundation, should foster a culture of physical and psychological safety, grace, growth through imperfection for truth learning, inquiry-based reasoning, and ultimately for personal and group improvement to be made possible.

Complementary to operating from the space of grace in community is the practice of humility and resiliency, with the latter of these amplifying the possibilities of learning from one's imperfections. Embracing imperfections provides space for community members to unlearn and to embrace new ways of thinking.

(Re)imagine and Truly Embrace DEIB in Curricula and Classroom Environments

When establishing community and learning curricula, hearing what others have to say is imperative. I differentiate listening from hearing by defining the latter as the ability to deeply and observingly pay attention to the iterations, intonation, subtext, context, and vocal cadence of the speakers' words. In this way, hearing allows the listeners to more deeply connect to the words, feelings, and thoughts of the speaker in an empathetic and process-oriented manner. Practicing hearing expands one's ability to extend grace alongside their sense of and need to protect the overall wellbeing of their fellow group members. Further, hearing allows for teachers and facilitators of learning to learn of the needs of students both inside and outside of class. The concept of hearing directly impacts one's ability to reason, consider, and adjust their course syllabi.

Often, however, most of us listen to respond. In this way, we do not hear what others are saying when they speak. Instead, many people center themselves and their personal thoughts by mentally disconnecting from the dialogue exchange and the needs of others. Other people will, for example, almost impatiently wait until the speaker finishes talking so they can center themselves by expressing what is on their minds regardless of the context offered by previous speakers. When people engage in dialogue from these perspectives, they are reducing the capacity in which they can show-up, care for, and support others. They are reducing their capacity to empathize. This, too, is atypical of inclusive community space-building practice. A challenge for us all in a fast-paced society is to hear one another, recognize, and honor another's humanity, and thus needs. I firmly believe that if we truly heard each other, we would express greater compassion and be a more peaceful, just, and equal society.

Students will have an increased likelihood of seeing themselves included, represented, and reflected in curricula when faculty members actively practice – and as senior leaders – wholly support heart and mind work. Homing in on justice as an expression of love, culturally responsive pedagogy, and teaching practices provides teachers and learning facilitators with the opportunity to engage students in conversation and curricula that centers on aspects of their cultural values, traditions, heritages, expressions, experiences, and identities.[18]

Defined by the educational philosopher Gloria Ladson-Billings, culturally responsive teaching is the theoretical approach to designing curricula and other teaching materials that ensure the following components are met: discipline-specific content for student learning and outcome purposes; cultural competence for students to better understand how and why an aspect of the course content matters at the individual level; and critical consciousness in support of students analyzing, critically thinking, and mapping the intersections of inequities, marginalization, and the otherwise mistreatment of groups of people by institutions and markers of society.[19]

Centering cultural competence within curriculum accelerates a class community's ability to fuse the mantra of shared ownership, equity, agency, and advocacy in teaching materials, as well as in the community space environment. Championing the art of hearing is fundamental to the approach of how teachers should design their curricula. As educators, we must be attuned to the needs of our students and to ourselves by ensuring our curricula allow for a multitude of perspectives, cultures, experiences, and skills.

Exercising the following principles is also central to the embodiment of inclusive curricula practices:

- Fuse empathy and equity to sustain community belonging.
- Express care, gratitude, grace, shared ownership, and vested interest in students learning opportunities, contributions, and achievements.
- Leverage student agency by learning of the content, wellness needs, and desires of students.
- Extend space and the opportunity for advocacy to students that enhance student-centered academic programs, institutional plans, and priorities.
- Support collaboration among faculty and students as the cornerstone of inclusion.
- Center writers, thinkers, artists, genres of varying identities, abilities, and expression mediums within the curriculum.
- Center an inclusive and substantively diverse cannon of preeminent thinkers and doers by highlighting their contributions to the discipline, including in- and out-of-class speaking engagements, course projects, research initiatives, and other works.
- Embrace EI.
- Empower others by extending support.

- Leverage the power of hearing.
- Remember that the sustaining of culturally inclusive environments is a journey of deep commitment, and that *we* are in this together.
- Remind yourself and others to operate from a space of grace.

Stay Encouraged on the Journey of Social Justice and Transformational Healing

No one gets everything right all the time. The truth is, we adjust how to engage with others based on their level, degree of, and energy toward the interaction. Thus, there will be moments when your approach to a conversation, issue, or concern differs. On some occasions, there will be times when you feel underprepared, unequipped, and unsure. In those moments remember that you have all the resources you need to support your students, engage in servant leadership, and provide shared-learning experience for learners authentically and lovingly. Nonetheless, if ever you find yourself full of doubt or uncertainty, I encourage you to read the below message I've crafted just for you:

> You're on the journey to transformational growth and realization, and I'm so proud of you. Tomorrow's class or lesson can very well be the beginning of a new and exciting era of your teaching tenure. Practicing community space-building grounded in love, truth, bravery, justice, and the transformative teachings of student agency and ownership are large yet worthwhile undertakings. As you venture ahead, remind yourself and your students that kindness goes a long way. Be kind to yourself and to others, for you all are on a journey of discovery. Everyone's views matter, and it's important to cultivate community so all viewpoints are heard and respected. Ask and receive feedback and suggestions with an open heart. Remember, this is not a power struggle. Everyone has capacity to own their learning and how they choose to engage in community. Listen with you heart, not just your ears. I believe in you. You've got this.
>
> Jasmine

Conclusion

In a polarizing society that has embraced anti-otherness alongside forms of physical violence rooted in the targeted marginalization, discrimination, harassment, and oppression of people, we must prioritize the work needed to build, foster, and sustain new, welcoming, and inclusive communities for the mental and physical safety of all people. Diversity, inclusion, equity, and belonging are four principles that guide and undergird the development of welcoming and supportive classrooms, institutional cultures, organizations, and environments. The foundation upon which inclusive community spaces – including learning and creative environments thrive – is based on the art and practice of community. The active practice of inclusive community space-building leads to heightened senses of trust, benevolence, belonging, support, care, value, and wellbeing. When this happens, students, faculty, and leaders alike find flourishing dynamics in which all people know they belong, are valued as individual and group contributors to their environment and are supported in ways both needed and desired. Engaging in the practice of heart and mind work while being rooted in grace and empathy advances the outcomes of the person-to-person connection by leveraging humanity and humility. As our nation continues to diversify, the increased adoption and embodiment of heart and mind practices will continue to enhance and lead to the development of inclusive, and equitably centered learning, living, community, and professional environments.

Notes

1 Jill Barshay, "College Students Predicted to Fall by More Than 15% after the Year 2025," The Hechinger Report, September 2018, access date November 21, 2021, https://hechingerreport.org/college-students-predicted-to-fall-by-more-than-15-after-the-year-2025/.
2 National Center for Educational Statistics, "Status and Trends in the Education of Racial and Ethnic Groups – Indicator 1: Population Distribution," Institute of Education Sciences, National Center for Educational Statistics, February 2019, access date August 26, 2021, https://nces.ed.gov/programs/raceindicators/indicator_raa.asp.
3 American Association of Colleges & Universities, "Facts & Figures: College Students Are More Diverse Than Ever Before. Faculty and Administrators Are Not," American Association of Colleges & Universities, March 2019, access date August 27, 2021, https://www.aacu.org/aacu-news/newsletter/2019/march/facts-figures.
4 U.S. Department of Education, "The Condition of Education 2020," Institute of Education Sciences, National Center for Educational Statistics, May 2020, access date August 26, 2021, https://nces.ed.gov/programs/coe/indicator/csc.
5 M. Scott Peck, *The Different Drum: Community Making and Peace* (New York: Touchstone Books, 2010), 59.
6 Brené Brown, *Braving the Wilderness: The Quest for True Belonging and the Courage to Stand Alone* (New York: Random House, 2017).
7 Martin Luther King, Jr., Where Do We Go from Here? Annual Report delivered by Dr. Martin Luther King, Jr., *11th Convention of the Southern Christian Leadership Conference*, August 16, 1967.

8 Bell hooks, *All About Love: New Visions* (New York: HarperCollins, 2000), 33.
9 Nell Noddings, *Education and Democracy in the 21st Century* (New York: Teachers College Press, 2013).
10 Brené Brown, "The Power of Vulnerability," TED, January 3, 2011, video, 20:49, https://youtu.be/iCvmsMzlF7o.
11 The framework in which I use "courage" is based on Brené Brown's January 2011 TED Talk titled *The Power of Vulnerability* wherein Brown noted that courage means to tell the story of who you are with your whole heart. More information on her articulation is provided here: https://youtu.be/iCvmsMzlF7o.
12 Zaretta Hammond, *Culturally Responsive Teaching and the Brain: Promoting Authentic Engagement and Rigor among Culturally and Linguistically Diverse Students* (Thousand Oaks: Corwin Press, 2015).
13 John D. Mayer, David R. Caruso, and Peter Salovey, "The Ability Model of Emotional Intelligence: Principles and Updates," *Emotion Review* 8, (2016): 1–11.
14 Bell hooks, *Teaching Community: A Pedagogy of Hope* (New York: Routledge, 2003).
15 Kerry Patterson, Joseph Grenny, David Maxfield, Ron McMillian, and Al Switzler, *Crucial Accountability: Tools for Resolving Violated Expectations, Broken Commitments, and Bad Behavior* (McGraw Hill Education: New York, 2013).
16 Paulo Friere, *Pedagogy of the Oppressed*, (New York: Continuum), 2000.
17 Cleo Wade, *Heart Talk: Poetic Wisdom for a Better Life* (Altria: New York, 2018).
18 Bettina Love, *We Want to do More Than Survive: Abolitionist Teaching and the Pursuit of Educational Freedom* (Boston: Beacon Press), 2020.
19 Gloria Ladson-Billings, "Toward a Theory of Culturally Relevant Pedagogy," *American Educational Research Journal* 32, no. 3 (1995): 478.

Bibliography

American Association of Colleges & Universities. "Facts & Figures: College Students Are More Diverse Than Ever Before. Faculty and Administrators Are Not." American Association of Colleges & Universities, March 2019. Access date August 27, 2021. https://www.aacu.org/aacu-news/newsletter/2019/march/facts-figures.

Barshay, Jill. "College Students Predicted to Fall by More Than 15% after the Year 2025." The Hechinger Report, September 2018. Access date November 22, 2021. https://hechingerreport.org/college-students-predicted-to-fall-by-more-than-15-after-the-year-2025/.

Brown, Brené. *Braving the Wilderness: The Quest for True Belonging and the Courage to Stand Alone*. New York: Random House, 2017.

Brown, Brené. "The Power of Vulnerability." TED, January 3, 2011, video, 20:49, https://youtu.be/iCvmsMzlF7o.

Friere, Paulo. *Pedagogy of the Oppressed*. New York: Continuum, 2000.

Hammond, Zaretta. *Culturally Responsive Teaching and the Brain: Promoting Authentic Engagement and Rigor Among Culturally and Linguistically Diverse Students*. Thousand Oaks: Corwin Press, 2015.

Hooks, Bell. *All About Love: New Visions*. New York: HarperCollins, 2000.

Hooks, Bell. *Teaching Community: A Pedagogy of Hope*. New York: Routledge, 2003.

King, Jr., Martin Luther. *Where Do We Go From Here?*, Annual Report delivered by Dr. Martin Luther King, Jr., 11th Convention of the Southern Christian Leadership Conference, August 16, 1967.

Ladson-Billings, Gloria. "Toward a Theory of Culturally Relevant Pedagogy," *American Educational Research Journal* 32, no. 3 (1995): 465–491.

Love, Bettina. *We Want to do More Than Survive: Abolitionist Teaching and the Pursuit of Educational Freedom*. Boston: Beacon Press, 2020.

Ma, Jennifer. "Trends and Issues: Recent Trends in Faculty Demographics and Employment Patterns." TIAA-CREF Institute, November 2004. Access date August 27, 2021. https://www.tiaainstitute.org/sites/default/files/presentations/2017-02/tr110104.pdf.

Mayer, John D., Caruso, David R., and Salovey, Peter. "The Ability Model of Emotional Intelligence: Principles and Updates." *Emotion Review* 8, (2016): 1–11.

National Center for Educational Statistics. "Status and Trends in the Education of Racial and Ethnic Groups – Indicator 1: Population Distribution." Institute of Education Sciences. National Center for Educational Statistics, February 2019. Access date August 26, 2021. https://nces.ed.gov/programs/raceindicators/indicator_raa.asp.

National Student Clearinghouse Research Center. "Benchmarks, Current Enrollment, Current Term Enrollment Estimates." NSC Research Center, June 10, 2021. Access date August 27, 2021. https://nscresearchcenter.org/current-term-enrollment-estimates/.

Noddings, Nell. *Education and Democracy in the 21st Century*. New York: Teachers College Press, 2013.

Patterson, Kerry, Grenny, Joseph, Maxfield, David, McMillian, Ron, and Switzler, Al. *Crucial Accountability: Tools for Resolving Violated Expectations, Broken Commitments, and Bad Behavior*. McGraw Hill Education: New York. 2013.

Peck, M. Scott. *The Different Drum: Community Making and Peace*. New York: Touchstone Books, 2010.

United States Census Bureau. "Quick Facts: United States." United States Census Bureau. United States Department of Commerce, 2019. Access date August 26, 2021. https://www.census.gov/quickfacts/fact/table/US/PST045219.

U.S. Department of Education. "The Condition of Education 2020." Institute of Education Sciences, National Center for Educational Statistics, May 2020. Access date August 26, 2021. https://nces.ed.gov/programs/coe/indicator/csc.

Wade, Cleo. *Heart Talk: Poetic Wisdom for a Better Life*. Altria: New York, 2018.

3 Embracing The 21st Century Superpowers of Creativity, Collaboration, Entrepreneurship, Adaptability, and Playfulness

Brian Pertl

Here we are, knee-deep in the 21st century, and music departments, music schools, and conservatories around the globe are scrambling to change curricula, expand training, and provide resources to create the elusive 21st century musician. Fantastic! But wait a second, here's a news flash: we have been graduating 21st century musicians and putting them out into the world for over 20 years, and still, at every conference and every gathering of music educators we are breathlessly trying to figure out how to best prepare our students for the 21st century. Shouldn't we have figured this out by now? What are we doing wrong? It's a big question that the entire field of music education should be thinking about. And, based on our past results, perhaps thinking about it in completely new ways.

We need to recognize and address the monumental disconnect between the true needs of a 21st century musician and the inability of most music institutions to fully address those needs. We can no longer make minor changes around the periphery of a predominantly unchanged system and hope that this will be enough to create a radically new kind of 21st century musician. Instead, we must reimagine the entire educational model and expand the very definition of high-level musicianship to include the high-level 21st century superpowers that music graduates will need to create a fulfilling and impactful musical life not just in the years immediately after graduation, but 10, 20, even 60-years into the future. The superpowers I am talking about are creativity, entrepreneurship, collaboration, adaptability, and playfulness. If we are serious about training true 21st century musicians, then we need to roll these superpowers into every aspect of our institutions and everything we do.

DOI: 10.4324/9781003218630-3

So why are these the ideal superpowers for the 21st century? Great question. Let's figure that out together. First, let's look at what challenges and opportunities have confronted musicians since the chronometer turned over to the year 2000; the birth of the 21st century. We will begin with technology. In 1999, on the eve of the 21st century, the peer-to-peer file-sharing platform, Napster was released. By 2000, Napster was shaking the very foundations of the music industry as millions of individuals began sharing their digital music collections directly, thereby bypassing any payment model to record companies, publishers, and artists. It signaled the eventual collapse of CD sales worldwide. What a way to kick off the century! Then iTunes launched in 2001. In 2003 Skype was released. Facebook launched in 2004. YouTube and Pandora hit the market in 2005, Twitter in 2006, Amazon Music in 2007, Bandcamp, SoundCloud, and Spotify in 2008, Instagram in 2010, Snapchat in 2011, Zoom in 2012, Apple Music in 2015, and TikTok in 2017. What new world-shaking applications will launch this year or next year? We can't be sure, but we know they are coming. So how do we prepare today's music students for technologies that don't yet exist?

Then there is the monumental shift in the accessibility, affordability, and overall quality of home recording and video production tools. In 2020, Billie Eilish won five Grammy Awards for an album she and her brother recorded in her bedroom and produced on his computer, signaling to the world that award-winning music can be made with minimal expense, far from high-end recording studios. Eilish's success illuminated limitless possibilities for the millions of musicians who could not previously afford to produce high-quality recordings. Coupled with the unprecedented availability of low-cost or no-cost distribution models, musicians can now release their music to the world in ways that were unthinkable at the start of this millennium. So, imagining the future our students will soon inherit, how do we train them to take full advantage of technological advances in recording and video production that don't yet exist?

The amount of change we have experienced since 2000 is impressive, even mind-blowing, but not wholly unexpected. We know that technology gets faster, cheaper, and more robust over time. So, while we can't predict exactly what technology will emerge and radically alter the music industry, we know that our lives will continue to be impacted by technological developments. Some changes, however, are not so easy to predict—enter the global pandemic.

In a matter of weeks, nearly every aspect of life was impacted by the pandemic. Lockdowns, masks, social distancing, gathering capacities, anxiety, fear, worry, isolation, illness, loss, grief, and death—the world turned upside down. There were also unexpected benefits—moments of stillness to reflect on what is truly important, time to listen in and listen out, silence to hear birdsong in the deserted streets of major cities, and space to grasp the critical importance of human connection. In a world that often frames music as mere entertainment or as a nice but dispensable indulgence, the pandemic forced us to re-think the central importance of our art form. In less time than it takes to pack up for a gig, all in-person music rehearsals, all in-person music performances, all in-person music teaching, and all in-person sharing of music in any way just stopped. Poof, gone, just like that. That monumental loss also reminded us of deep and powerful truths about our art:

Music is magic.

Music is medicine.
Music is food for the soul.
Music is the bringer of joy.
Music is the balm for sorrow.
Music is a human need.

The pandemic also forced musicians to confront the realities of a musical world where face-to-face music-making was a practical impossibility. And a twin reality: the economic and professional collapse foisted upon performing musicians. So how do we prepare our music students to handle unpredictable, catastrophic events that impact nearly every aspect of our field?

On May 25th, 2020, just weeks after the world was flung headlong into the realities of a global pandemic, the public, televised murder of George Floyd sparked global protests, focusing unprecedented attention on systemic racism throughout Western society. Many music schools were quick to acknowledge the systemic racism, elitism, and exclusionary practices within their walls. They took this moment to begin a conversation about systemic racism in our music programs and asked how music programs might become a positive force for creating more diverse, equitable, and inclusive institutions and societies. A re-energized Black Lives Matter movement proved to be a powerful catalyst for institutions to start reshaping the Western classical music institutions: from auditions to access, curriculum and repertoire, audience engagement, and performance practice. This monumental re-imagining has just begun in earnest, although the breadth of opportunities for today's musicians to re-think and recreate and revitalize Western classical music ecosystems is practically unlimited. And to be clear, there is nothing more important for the future of Western classical music than to become systemically diverse, inclusive, equitable, and actively anti-racist. So how do we train our music students to be change-leaders in positioning music, including Western classical music, at the forefront of diversity, equity, inclusion, and anti-racism efforts?

These enormous questions bring us back to where we started: why are we still having so much trouble figuring out how to train the 21st century musician? Reframed: in a world of constant change, why wouldn't we struggle in figuring out how to train the ideal 21st century musician? It feels like a constant game of catch-up. How can we possibly prepare young graduates to leverage emerging technologies and overcome systemic uncertainty if we can't see into the future?

Had we only known a global pandemic would confine the world's population to their home, we might have added courses in Pedagogy for Online Private Lessons, Maximizing Web Rehearsal Efficiency, Programming and Producing Compelling Web Concerts, and Creating Asynchronous Ensemble Recordings. These courses would have proved super helpful for our 2019 graduates. But wait, these courses would have been super helpful for our 2018 and 2017 graduates, too. Hold on though, these classes would have been valuable for our 2001 graduates. They too had to figure out how to navigate the pandemic. But even if, in 2001, we could have forecast a global pandemic in 2020, the technology used to connect us during the pandemic hadn't yet been invented. Hmmm.

But hang on, what about our 1990s graduates and 1980s graduates, and 1970s graduates? I received my undergraduate degree in the mid-80s. I was still using a typewriter for my assignments. No one was thinking about email let alone zero-latency distanced ensemble rehearsals. But I too am a 21st century musician. If you are reading this, you are a 21st century musician too, no matter what year you graduated or will graduate. So, we are still scrambling to figure out how to train a 21st century musician, because the *now* of the 21st century is in constant flux.

If we focus too much on providing specific tools to handle the challenges and opportunities that exist in the *now*, we get caught looking down at our feet instead of 50 miles down the road. Yes, we need to be acutely aware of the musical ecosystems our graduates will enter upon leaving our institutions. But we also need to provide the tools that will maximize their success far into the future. How amazingly beautiful would it have been if my professors in the 1980s were steadfastly committed to providing me with 21st century musical skills? How amazingly cool would it be if today's music schools were steadfastly committed to training graduates for 2075?

This is where our 21st century superpowers come in. Creativity, entrepreneurship, collaboration, adaptability, and playfulness are the superpowers that transcend time and prepare a musician to take-on technologies not yet invented, opportunities not yet dreamed of, and unknown challenges not yet encountered. Before we discuss these superpowers, let's never forget that our graduates still need a high-level technical and musical ability. 21st century musicians need chops. You need chops if you are a performer. You need chops if you are a music educator. You need chops if you are an arts administrator. There are no shortcuts to the time, effort, intentionality, and thought required to reach true musical mastery. What I am also saying is that the potential of the 21st century musician is fully realized when the technical facility and deep musicality are completely integrated with creativity, entrepreneurship, collaboration, adaptability, and playfulness. For the ideal 21st century musician, these skills and traits are all part of the same whole.

Creativity stands as the key superpower for a musician facing the ever-changing challenges of today and tomorrow's world; creativity as a way of life, creativity as a force that can solve intractable problems or conjure new opportunities in every aspect of a musician's journey. A truly creative person is always asking "why." Why does a classical music recital look and sound the way it does? Why don't more people attend our heart-wrenchingly beautiful classical music performances? Why is there so little diversity in major symphony orchestras? Looking at every aspect of the world and asking "why" allows us to see the world in new ways. When you stop seeing things as inevitable and start seeing things as dynamic possibilities for change, the world becomes less fixed. You begin to occupy the magical world of the liminal, neither here nor there, where infinite possibilities abound. It might be uncomfortable at first. Uncertainty often is. But it is within this liminal space where "aha" moments burst into existence. A 21st century musician who brings true creativity to every aspect of their lives possesses the means to pivot, change course, and see opportunities where others see only roadblocks. When you have no idea what the future holds, creativity illuminates a path forward.

Composers and improvisers have likely experienced the exhilaration of being in the liminal world of creative flow when time is suspended, and music pours forth. There is only the now the music and you. The creativity experienced in music composition may be very different from the creativity experienced in generating a new business idea, or in inventing a new approach to virtual recitals, but in each instance, creativity is key to bringing to life something that didn't exist before.

What if you could leverage that creative flow for everything you do and every challenge you face? Wow. Pretty powerful stuff. If I were to gift one trait to every musician that would aid them in overcoming the unknown challenges of tomorrow, next year, or forty years from now, it would be virtuosic creativity. Once we accept creativity as a meta-power that can be applied to art, business, or life; once we realize liminal spaces hold magical creative potential for all facets of our being; once we realize that creativity doesn't divide our existence into discrete areas, but unifies our existence into unlimited collaborative potential, then we are ready to face the challenges and opportunities of today and of the future. In fact, all other superpowers discuss in this chapter flow out of the wellspring of creativity.

Collaboration is the second great superpower. Musicians understand the power of collaboration. There is nothing quite like making music with others. There are unspoken bonds that form between musicians as they play together. There is also collaboration in making music *for* others. Performers and audiences become connected, exchanging energy and emotion. Creating community and building community is central to music-making. Collaboration is a catalyst that can supercharge creativity. As an individual, it is gratifying to get into the creative flow, but collaborative creativity can take everything to the next level. Collaborative improvisation with musicians who are co-occupying a liminal creative space can lead to experiences that are nothing short of mind-blowing. Think of a jazz combo creating a free improvisation where every member is in the creative flow. Musical ideas mesh and merge and intersect in ways that are impossibly complex, deeply moving, and seemingly magical. The same kind of approach to collaborative improvisation can be used to tackle challenges or opportunities in any sphere.

High-level collaborative improvisation to dream up new business possibilities? Why not? Why can't we see business meetings or committee meetings as jam sessions where we riff off one another, listen deeply, hold space, fill space, and complete each other's thoughts? Reaching that place of pure collaborative magic is rare, and the more collaborators you have, the trickier it is to have everyone enter the sacred liminality at once. But it is possible. And absolutely worth the effort. The more you do it, the easier it gets. Your success as a musician increases exponentially when you have collaborators who are willing to jam with you in every aspect of your musical life.

So how do you begin incorporating collaborative improvisation into business meetings, committee work, board meetings, Western classical string quartet rehearsals, or any other situation that feels like it would be the last place on earth a jam session might otherwise take place? Start by asking yourself why the situation feels like the last place on earth the freedom of playful improvisation might spontaneously occur. I imagine for most of us, nearly every meeting environment feels antithetical to spontaneous improvisation. Detailed agendas, long-standing expectations, well-established protocols, and the status quo can all conspire to keep things exactly as they've always been. After all, the reason we all dread going to long boring meetings is because we have such clear expectations that meetings are, by definition, long and boring. Our expectations help create the very atmosphere we so dread. So, let's turn all that on its head.

Agendas, expectations, protocols, and the status quo are not inherently bad, nor do they inherently suppress creativity. Let's create new agendas, new expectations, new protocols, and a new status quo that normalizes a culture of jamming! Start small and create a climate that allows colleagues to safely venture out of their comfort zones. Add time to the agenda for collaborative improvisation at every meeting. Create an expectation that every meeting will include something unexpected, something that will shake things up, and compel attendees to interact with one another collaboratively. Create a culture that helps teach openness and risk-taking. What if a faculty meeting started with a 5-minute collaborative movement session led by a dance professor? What if an agenda item to solve an intractable problem started with 5 minutes of freewriting while listening to music? And then moved into collaborative small group brain flurries before coming back together for a full-blown brainstorm? There is no single right way to create an immersive culture of collaborative improvisation. What is certain, however, is that collaborative cultures can only happen when you intentionally embed them within everything you do.

The superpower of entrepreneurship – or an entrepreneurial mindset – can also be thought of as business creativity. We often think of business as the opposite of the arts. And business practice as the opposite of artistic practice. But why can't business practice be as creative as artistic practice? What might be possible if we were to embrace the same creative flow experienced while composing or improvising when envisioning a new business model or marketing strategy?

When running their business, 21st century musicians need to be wildly entrepreneurial. Why? Because the business you'll be running is the business of you and your art. And it's unlikely that it will be just one business, but rather a multi-faceted business conglomerate. If you haven't yet thought of your musical career in those terms, perhaps you should. Here are some of the micro-businesses most musicians juggle: free-lance performer, ensemble musician, studio teacher, classroom teacher, event organizer, composer and arranger, marketer, and webmaster. Then there is strategic planning, budgeting, and tax preparation. Yikes! That's a lot. *Being a musician is about as business-y a business as a business can be.* That's why an entrepreneurial mindset is so darn important for navigating a musical life in an ever-changing world.

The field of arts entrepreneurship emerged in the 1990s and continues to extend its reach well into the 21st century. And although scholars offer diverse approaches to entrepreneurial thinking and action, what is shared across the field of thought is that entrepreneurs begin with curiosity, as they seek to identify problems they are uniquely equipped to solve, creativity for finding new ways to combine and connect ideas, and collaboration for building teams equal to the challenge. Many of the traits held by successful entrepreneurs align surprisingly well with traits indicative of successful musicians. Resiliency, tenacity, and the ability to overcome failure are essential to both entrepreneurs and musicians. A successful musician is also an expert storyteller, weaving a compelling tale through music. A compelling performance allows the audience to feel even the most nuanced emotion. Similarly, entrepreneurs must tell the story of their big, bold idea in such a way that potential collaborators, funders, and clients can clearly see and even feel the beauty of their entrepreneurial dream. One challenge for our aspiring 21st century musicians is to realize that their musical training has already given them so many foundational skills needed to be an entrepreneur.

Sometimes, however, our musical and entrepreneurial skillsets do not naturally align. Successful entrepreneurs understand from the outset the importance of funding entrepreneurial enterprises. Many musicians find the idea of budgeting and financial planning foreign, and even slightly terrifying. We fear the world of finance because we have no familiarity with it. It is very hard to be creative, innovative, and forward-looking in areas that one fears. Yet it is impossible to be a successful entrepreneur without knowledge of, and comfort with, finances. If a sustainable financial plan is all that stands between a young musical entrepreneur and a dream of implementing an arts program that will positively impact a community, or a dream of creating affordable instruments that will allow thousands more young people to participate in music-making, or a dream of creating a successful virtual music school, then we need to add financial facility to every musicians core skillset, right alongside sight-singing, aural skills, keyboard training, and all the rest. Our musicians need to be comfortable enough with budgeting and finances so that they can implement a financial model that will allow their beautiful artistic ideas to become realities.

Adaptability is the fourth superpower. Adaptability is a willingness to grow, try new things, and learn new skills, even when it's slightly terrifying to do so. Adaptability is a critical 21st Century superpower. Since the world is constantly changing and new opportunities require new skills, possessing the curiosity to learn, the willingness to dive-in, and the adaptability to flex are vital, when taking-on new artistic ventures.

We need to equip life-long learners open to learning new skills. This could be learning how to build websites, produce high-quality videos, or maximize social media presence. It could also be learning a new instrument, developing acting chops, or venturing into songwriting. It absolutely means exploring new genres and venturing into new cross-disciplinary collaborations.

Often, when we talk about adaptability and the willingness to quickly change directions, the presumption is that the truly agile musician already possesses the skills necessary for successfully navigating the new course. Vastly, this is not true. In reality, successful individuals see opportunity, recognize new skills required to take full advantage of the opportunity, and then commit themselves to learning these skills.

Leila Ramagopal Pertl–forward-thinking leader in Music Education, sought after expert in infusing equity, diversity, and inclusion into music education, and truly extraordinary life partner (yes, it is my great fortune to be married to this remarkable leader) – sums it up for her students with this advice: "Never be afraid to be a beginner." It is simple to say, but often harder to put into practice.

Diving into new learning challenges should never be seen as a burden, but rather embraced for the miraculous potential it holds for unexpected life-changing adventures. To realize adaptability's full potential as a superpower, we must recognize that musicianship is not synonymous with an instrument you play. Your instrument is just one conduit for your musicality to emerge into the world. The genre of music you are most comfortable playing is just one conduit of your musical self. When you reimagine your musical identity as one no longer defined by the instrument you play, but rather the culmination of your musical, creative, adaptable self, then any instrument, genre, collaboration, pedagogy, or performance opportunity is a conduit for expressing what the world needs most—the beautiful, transformational music found uniquely within you. For this to be achieved, however, requires our final superpower: playfulness.

Can playfulness really be a superpower? Yes, playfulness is a superpower. That is if it's the right kind of playfulness. Musicians play all the time. We play our instruments. We play music. We play with other musicians. For most of us, however, this kind of play has little to do with the superpower of playfulness.

Sadly, in a musical context, the word "play" is usually pragmatic, even mundane. I play the trombone. I play in a band. Playfulness as a superpower is all about the wonder, magic, engagement, and infinite potential that we associate with children at play. Why? Because play has everything to do with creativity, collaboration, and fully occupying the present moment. Play is dancing in the liminal. Play is imagining new worlds that have never existed before. Play is suspending time while you are creating in the *now*. Play can be joyful and wild and loud. Play can be focused and quiet and introspective. Play is the serious business of creative problem-solving. Musicians who can reintroduce the concept of play into playing music, into creating a business, and into creating a musical life, have a distinct advantage in a world where the landscape is always changing. We musicians need to reclaim the magical potential of the word "play." Virtuoso trombonist, composer, and Deep Listener, Stuart Dempster, says that his goal is to put the playback into playing music. If we want to nurture the superpower of playfulness, we should make this our goal as well.

If the world needs creative, collaborative, entrepreneurial, adaptable, and playful musicians – and it does – then we need to ask ourselves: what type of music school is best equipped to empower our musical superheroes? I would argue that it would be a school that possesses those exact same qualities: the Creative, Collaborative, Entrepreneurial, Adaptable, Playful School of Music. It has a nice ring to it, wouldn't you agree? Where can I sign up? But seriously, how many music schools do you know fit this description?

Offering a course, or courses in entrepreneurship is a good start. But that doesn't make a school entrepreneurial. Offering courses in composition and improvisation is fantastic. But it doesn't make the school inherently creative. Sadly, most institutions are closer to The Unchanging, Pragmatic, Steadfast, Serious School of Music. And how many of us are ready to sign-up for that?

How effective can this brand of music school be in fostering students' 21st century superpowers? Truthfully, it can't. It is the equivalent of building a high-tech, futuristic car in Henry Ford's new-fangled, 1913 factory. Obviously, musicians aren't machines fresh off an assembly line, but if we are trying to produce the ideal 21st century musician, equipped with requisite superpowers with an educational structure firmly rooted in the early 19th century, we are doomed to fail.

Arguing that we are doing our best, we make changes around the edges. Yet we continue to fail our music students on their journeys to invent the future they will soon inherit. To change we need to recognize two important truths about music schools and emerging musicians:

- Course focusing on 21st century superpowers sprinkled throughout the curriculum will not make creativity, entrepreneurship, collaboration, adaptability, and playfulness central to the music school's core identity.
- And emerging musicians will only grow their 21st century superpowers consistently and fully when school ecosystems embed creativity, entrepreneurship, collaboration, adaptability, and playfulness within the institutional DNA.

Recognizing and addressing the monumental disconnect between emerging musicians' needs for 21st century training and music schools' willingness and ability (or unwillingness and inability) to prioritize these superpowers is the grand challenge facing music in higher education today. We need to stop making changes around the peripheries of an unchanging educational model and begin radically reimagining the entire educational model built upon a foundation of creativity, entrepreneurship, collaboration, adaptability, and playfulness.

What problems – beyond 150 years of resistance to change on nearly every front – do we face?

We have a veneration problem. We have enshrined the myth of Western European classical music's supremacy. Anchoring the argument that the very nature of Western classical music is infallible and unchanging, we've deified classical music's canon – defined by the all-white, all-male, all-dead, "genius composer." This veneration compels our music education models to remain fixed and unchanging. Consequently, too often the fierce, searing, transformational beauty of Western classical music is muted by its culture and exclusion.

We have a legacy problem in academia. Our professoriate studied diligently under their professors, who were devoted students of their faculty, who were, inevitably protégés of mythical titans with classical music's lineage (Think: Johannes Brahms, Frédéric Chopin, Nadia

Boulanger). These musical genealogies of revered teacher-scholars preserve the status quo and solidify a legacy of pedagogy often at odds with our 21st century superpowers. How can a professor teach creativity through improvisation when they've never improvised and have no pedagogical grounding in creativity? Ironically, nearly all our Western classical music revered heroes were virtuosic improvisers, inventive composers, and masters of creativity. Hmm. Maybe we need to focus our educational models on these wildly creative aspects of Western classical music's legacy.

We have a bureaucracy problem in academia. Everything about the academic model resists rapid change. Shared governance, standing committees, faculty meetings, consensus building, and accrediting bodies are all wonderful tools for creating thoughtful, considered, thoroughly debated decisions. They, too, are also effective in suppressing change and ensuring that if change does happen, it is slowed to a glacial pace—not the hallmark of entrepreneurial agility. In colleges and universities, "fast-tracking" a new major or degree program usually means it will *only* take a year or two to be fully implemented.

For far too long, we've grown far too comfortable with an unchanging model. And our profound lack of urgency in preparing students for thriving careers in music harms our students and our profession. So how do we flip this legacy on its head when everything about this legacy does not want to be flipped on its head?

First, the timing for The Great Flipping couldn't be better. Ten years ago, The Great Flipping would have been nothing more than a dream. Even two years ago, change would have been iffy at best. Although the task is still monumental, today it is feasible. What's changed? A global pandemic and re-energized Black Lives Matter movement.

The pandemic demanded that the stoically unchanging world of classical music training – like it or not – must change *absolutely everything*. In a period of two weeks, Music schools in the United States and around the world migrated to complete distanced learning. This required learning new technologies, teaching from home offices, adapting news pedagogies, adjusting course syllabi, reimagining recitals, private lessons, ensemble rehearsals, chamber music coaching, and hundreds of other changes, big and small, that touched every area of our practice. Never have we witnessed such a profound and pervasive sense of urgency to take immediate action within a music education system that had grown comfortable moving at a glacial pace. Sweeping and instantaneous, the changes proved to music schools that they could do something they've historically failed to do: *they pivoted*.

Did you see that? I just used a business term in a book about music. In business, "to pivot" means to rapidly change your business model when it is no longer productive. That is exactly what happened. Music schools pivoted for the first time in our lifetimes. Granted, they were forced to pivot, but that does not detract from what we accomplished. Why? Because it showed us that radical, sweeping change was not only possible but wasn't nearly as disastrous as our pre-pandemic, curmudgeonly selves had feared.

In the dark, musty, unchanging hallways of music schools across the land, the pivot cracked open the door of possibility and allowed the bright light from the liminal land of "what if" to flood into our corridors. And with that door cracked open, another Earth-shaking event occurred.

The Black Lives Matter movement marked a tipping point in America's response to racial injustice. Millions of people in cities across America and around the globe took to the streets to protest police killings and the systemic racism that has brutalized BIPOC people in America every day and in every facet of life. There were unprecedented calls to address social injustice and systemic racism from every segment of society. And the urgency sweeping the globe swept across college campuses and into music programs. Students, faculty, and staff were compelled to act.

Now, with the Door of Infinite Possibility kicked open by the abrupt pivot to distance learning, faculty, staff, and students were creating a pivot of their own making with the knowledge that they were equipped to manage radical change. And that our seemingly unchanging, monolithic model for music education could withstand radical change.

What better time than now to dream the Creative, Collaborative, Entrepreneurial, Adaptable, Playful Music School into existence? A School built upon a foundation of systemic equity, systemic diversity, and systemic belonging.

Now that we know we can withstand and even drive change, let's get to the part where I tell you what classes you need to offer and what boxes you need to check to become a fully certified Creative, Entrepreneurial, Collaborative, Adaptable, Playful School of Music; a school that can expertly prepare creative, entrepreneurial, collaborative, adaptable, playful musical superheroes for the 21st century!

Sorry, that's just not going to happen. That goes against the fundamental notion of what we are building here. Just as we strive to empower every student to find their unique musical voice, we need to empower every music school to find its unique voice and the institutional identity that sets it apart from every other program.

The world does not need to franchise the CECAP School of Music. The diversity of programs across the United States and around the globe should be celebrated. The greater the diversity among institutional personalities equals the greater opportunities we've created to serve the diverse needs of aspiring 21st century musicians.

Rather, crafting your institution's unique identity will be a process of discovery involving stakeholders from every corner of your community. Where do we begin? With curiosity, of course. Be radically open. And ask questions.

What sets your program apart from all others?

What kind of students thrive there?

How might the unique histories of the community in which the program resides, help inform the identity of your school?

Is the program situated amidst a bustling urban environment where experiential learning opportunities are abundant? Or might rich regional traditions set the tone?

Let your imagination explore the infinite possibilities of whom you might become. And be wildly open to everything you hear and learn.

When you feel you have a good grip on your institution's unique identity and the influences of the community in which you reside, next ask the question: what do you want to become? This is a big, bold question that should evoke some big, bold dreaming.

Encourage individuals to imagine the ideal version of your music program. Hold space for student voices. Have community members free-write as many ideas as they can. There are no wrong answers. Let the pencil be a direct conduit for the magnificent creative power of the mind. Then host jam sessions for small groups of students, faculty, and staff to playfully riff off each other in the liminal space of possibility, holding space to listen, taking space to contribute, and occupying the now. Have fun. Be playful.

Look what we just did. Even during the first step of defining our current institutional identity and formulating our aspirational institutional identity, we used the superpowers of creativity, entrepreneurially thinking, collaboration, adaptability, and playfulness. Let that sink in for a moment. Students, faculty, the staff, and the entire music school community, began incorporating 21st century superpowers within their institutional culture even before we got to the point of asking, "so how do we incorporate 21st century superpowers into our institutional culture?" Yes. That's exactly what we did. And yes, it's that easy to start rolling these superpowers into every aspect of your community. And yes, it is that necessary, beautiful, and empowering to steep every aspect of your institutional identity in creativity, entrepreneurship, collaboration, adaptability, and play.

When the superpowers you aspire to nurture within your students are also part of the institutional DNA, then success isn't dependent on out-of-reach resources, ultra-modern facilities, or trendy guest speakers. It isn't even dependent on your programming. These attributes can be nurtured in programs exclusively dedicated to Western classical orchestral training, or programs dedicated to new music, jazz, hip hop, or improvisation. These superpowers can be rolled into musicology, music theory, and composition. Drawing upon the expansive creative resources of each community member and of the community's collective creativity, the possibilities are infinite.

So, does this mean we shouldn't be expanding our course offerings in entrepreneurship, improvisation, composition, interdisciplinary arts, dance, songwriting, jazz, hip hop, Brazilian Samba, Balinese gamelan, filmmaking, or the limitless ways of acquiring forward-thinking skills? Of course not! Each music program, depending on its own unique vision, personality, and focus should create courses that are specifically designed to build 21st century skills within their institution. Just remember that stand-alone courses are great, but not nearly enough. If we are serious about turning skills into superpowers, then we need to roll creativity, entrepreneurship, collaboration, adaptability, and playfulness into who we are as an institution.

What mixed messages are we sending students if we tell them that an entrepreneurial mindset is essential for a 21st century musician, but the only person in their music school actively demonstrating entrepreneurial attributes is their entrepreneurship professor? The situation would be further exacerbated if the only time a student practices entrepreneurial thinking is in the entrepreneurship course. It is ridiculous if you think about it, but for many schools, this scenario isn't far from reality. Instead, we need to make our superpowers an integral part of how we as a community walk, or rather dance, through life.

I know what you're thinking. "This sounds great on paper, but seriously, my community isn't going to buy into this. Have you met my sarrusophone professor? He has been teaching the exact same curriculum for the past 40 years and is still grumbling about the addition of jazz to our music program!" OK, not everyone is going to take ownership from day one. But don't write people off either. After all, Professor Sarrusophone pivoted to online teaching just like the rest of the faculty. And chances are, he changed more than a few aspects of the pedagogy in the process.

Don't underestimate the power of an ecosystem of creativity, play, and possibility. It will take time to reach a critical mass. But when 21st century superpowers are baked into your community, an electric, magical energy will permeate your building. The physical and the liminal space will co-exist. The air shimmering with creative possibilities. When you get to that point, the magic is infectious, and even your most curmudgeonly community members will begin to dance and play—behind closed doors at first. They have a reputation to uphold, after all. This is your sign that your ecosystem has been transformed.

Making creativity a core value throughout our institution requires us to redefine how we think about creativity. Society at large has an odd relationship with creativity. Businesses purport that they value creativity above all other attributes within corporate leaders. Corporations bombard employees with slide decks that tell them to be creative, innovative, and "think outside of the box."

Outwardly nodding affirmatively, employees inwardly are terrified that they just aren't creative enough to think outside of that proverbial box. Meanwhile, corporations occupy employees' mind space with endless training on everything from maximizing the power of spreadsheets and implementing cloud-based communication strategies, to leading productive teams and developing high-level negotiation tactics, but offer no training geared toward optimizing the power to think outside of the box.

What? Corporations place the highest value on creative, innovative leaders yet provide no training to grow creative, innovative leadership? None? But why? Historically, Western European-influenced cultures have held a deep belief that people are either creative or not. Musical, or not. Artistic, or not. It isn't that corporations are debating whether creativity training would be valuable or have a high return on investment (ROI). It's that conversation surrounding creativity training never happens because creativity is understood as a fixed asset from birth rather than a skill to be developed.

It may come as a surprise that music education suffers from this same misconception, even though creativity is so closely associated with musicians. Musicians may feel that their training is steeped in creativity, yet, when considering the 2 – 6 hours a day that they spend in the practice room, what percentage of that time is devoted to developing their musical creativity?

In our entrepreneurship classes, we tell our students to think-outside-the-box as a way of developing innovation and creativity. But how much time do we carve out for them to *practice* creativity? In musicology and theory are we encouraging our students to find new ways to make creative connections across disciplinary boundaries? Apart from composition and improvisation courses, are we baking in creativity development into the curriculum? Into the culture? We need to do better. So, let's make a change.

We first need to embrace the truth that creativity is our birthright, and we aren't given an arbitrary creativity quota at birth. If we practice creativity, we become ever more creative. How cool would it be for our 21st century musicians to possess both musical and creative virtuosity? Next, we must recognize that true creativity needs space to dance and play and fly. In a world that values busy-ness, multi-tasking, over-commitment, doing more, doing more faster, (and then feeling guilty about not doing enough); a world where every break is filled with emails, chats, social media, mobile devices, and news feeds, we need to hold space for creativity to flourish.

Busy-ness is the arch-enemy of creativity.

Start tilling the soil in which you will grow your creativity culture by embracing the mantra "do less, be more." Institutionally, you can start sending clear messages that doing less is a core value. Making this an institutional value is important because often our music school communities have an unspoken value of uplifting busy-ness. We inadvertently host the Busy-ness Olympics, where students, faculty, and staff vie for Gold for being the busiest of all.

Have ever overheard a conversation where one student says something like, "I just did two recitals, three concerts, turned in a 10-page research paper, and still have a community engagement project to finish. I haven't slept in 2-days." And another student replies, "Well if you think that's bad," and then does their best to out-busy the first student, you are witnessing the Busy-ness Olympics, and you have a busy-ness problem. Don't feel bad, and don't think you're alone. Every school has a busy-ness problem. But take a stand. Do less! Be more! We need to clear space for our creativity to flourish.

So, let's make space for creativity to flourish in every area of our programs. I call this space *ponder time*. The word "ponder" has a certain relaxed quality that helps set this time apart from the frantic pace of our busy lives. (You can call it whatever you want, be creative.) Ponder time isn't meditation. You aren't trying to clear your mind. You aren't focusing on your breathing. Ponder time provides room for your mind to be playful, dance, and make connections in the liminal space of possibility and wonder. You are making space for "aha" moments and new ideas. If you doubt the power of ponder time, think about how many great ideas have come to you in the shower. Showering *is* ponder time. Your tech is turned off. You aren't being bombarded by commitments and obligations. And the soaping and washing and rinsing are on autopilot, freeing your brain to do what it does best: tumble and play and make connections across everything you've been studying, practicing, and, well, pondering. During ponder time your mind is dancing in the liminal. It's romping and playing and puzzling things out. In those moments you are practicing creative thinking.

So how might we best practice ponder time? For me the approach to ponder time is open. No tech. But you can draw or doodle or freewrite. Ponder time can be practiced in a quiet space or a noisy café. You can take a walk. You can think about a problem you have been working on. Or you can just see what comes up in your mind. Some ponder times will end with exciting revelations. And some end with nothing happening at all. And that's OK. Part of practicing creativity is not trying to force creativity.

I require 20-minutes of daily ponder time from the students in my entrepreneurship class. And the students in my Deep Listening class. And my Roots Music class. And for that matter, every student in every one of my classes. Because if creativity is a 21st century superpower, shouldn't we be practicing creativity *all the time?* Shouldn't we require it from all of our students? And yes, I realize that "requiring" creativity seems counterintuitive to the freedom creativity demands. But in a world where busy-ness is revered, it is hard to make space on one's own for what might feel like the indulgence of doing nothing. Requiring ponder time for a class gives students the curricular cover to make space in their day to dream, guilt-free. After all, it's a requirement! Once they get a taste for making time for their mind to play, they will start making time for it on their own. This is true for faculty and staff, too. Ponder time should be a requirement for everyone if we are to build ecosystems of creativity that span our community.

Ponder time is just one way of spreading a culture of creativity throughout your community.

What if we were to apply a similar approach to musical creativity? Our students and performance faculty practice their instruments 2 – 6 hours a day. How might we foster musical creativity if we were to reallocate 10 – 20-minutes of each practice session to the musical equivalent of ponder time? And how might this particularly benefit classical musicians who otherwise have little or no experience with improvisation? What if studio teachers required 10 – 20-minutes of daily sonic exploration – required improv. I'm not talking about playing over the changes to *Giant Steps* or realizing figured bass lines, at least not at first. Instead, I'm talking about slowly building a personal creative relationship with your instrument and affording a freer exploration of musical possibilities: a sonic equivalent of ponder time.

For musicians who have never improvised this could be terrifying. So, add constraints that ease your way into the creative flow. Find the note that best expresses how you are feeling right now. What is the right volume and timbre? Take the first three pitches from a piece you are working on and use only those pitches to play an improvised mini-composition that expresses the personality of your dog, or cat, or fish, or your favorite stuffed animal. Play a memory of your favorite place. The possibilities are limitless. The most important part is to realize that practicing creativity is developing a vital superpower. This isn't just "noodling around." Creativity and playfulness are serious business.

Creating space for musicians to truly express their own musical voice is something that is sorely missing from most music programs. Think about the incredible creative potential that would be unleashed if every student incorporated 20-minutes of serious creative play into each practice session. That's 2-hours a week, 60-hours a year, and 240-hours over four years—that equals an entire month of 8-hour creativity practice sessions! Wow! Can you imagine what musical pathways students would create? Over time they could be improvising entire compositions based on a single idea or emotion or recomposing pieces they are working on. Not just writing one's own cadenza but improvising a cadenza incorporating the feelings and emotions of the moment.

There is of course more scaffolding required for developing competency in improvisation – and boundless resources on the market – but my hope is to excite within you the power of the idea. The other beautiful thing about this approach is that professors don't have to have expertise in improvisation. Instead, they only need to afford themselves the opportunity to take the creative journey right alongside their students. Building comfort for exploring creativity for everyone in our community opens up a magical world of possibility and connection and will likely empower students (and maybe some faculty) to take formal courses in improvisation and composition, or explore improvisational musical traditions like jazz, or free improv, or …Western classical music.

Up to this point, our focus has been on nurturing the creative impulse within the individual: increasing their comfort level to dance and play and dream in the liminal spaces both intellectually and musically. Now imagine what might be possible if every member of your musical community – students, staff, and faculty – were committed to the daily practice of creative growth. I'm going to hit the pause button so that you can take a moment to imagine what it would be like to be a part of this community of creators.

Are you imagining the enormous creative potential of this community? The electricity of a space filled with people primed to dream, imagine, and create? A community that welcomes every person to occupy the liminal space of not knowing exactly what comes next? Imagining is the first step toward infusing creativity into the DNA of your institution.

It's fascinating to know that fostering a community devoted to creativity doesn't require us to add a single course or degree program. But this is only a small piece of a much more powerful manifestation of our 21st century superpowers. Remember the superpower of collaboration? Add collaborative creativity to the scene and we've just gone from black and white to ultra-high-definition Technicolor. In the world of today and tomorrow and 20 years from now, every entrepreneurial venture and musical opportunity will involve high-level collaboration. And wielding your superpowers in collaborative creativity will prove to be critical to your success.

So, while we are nurturing individual creativity within our music schools, we also need to create endless opportunities for nurturing collaborative creativity. And we can do that by taking the same approach as before: leveraging existing spaces, both physical and temporal, to grow collaborative creativity and embed it in our institutional DNA.

At the beginning of my entrepreneurship class – every class, all term – I guide students through a Deep Listening group-improvisation. Critically important, is my own participation. By taking part, I position myself as a co-explorer and co-creator alongside my students, instead of the "all-knowing" professor. These group improvisations involve singing together or moving together. And two things are always true: 1) participants learn to become intimately aware of everyone's contributions and 2) participants learn how to be appropriately responsive to the actions of others.

Together, we learn to listen, hold space, and fill space. Together, we become an ensemble that fully occupies the liminal space. Not easy. Slightly terrifying. Often transcendently beautiful. Sometimes there is laughter that melts into music. Laughter? Is music-making supposed to be joyful, playful, and even funny?

The piece ends when the class moves from actively sounding together to collaboratively discovering an ending point: evidence of how deeply connected and in-tune a group of co-creators can become. Often the ending has a miraculous quality of its own. As if an invisible conductor gave a cut-off. Then, we occupy that energy-filled, electric silence that follows, basking in that magical absence of sound as a community. Although it may seem counterintuitive, there is a strong musical connection in that silence.

How long has it been since you've experienced this kind of connective, collaborative playfulness in your music-making?

After we finish, I always ask students, "What did that have to do with entrepreneurship?" Not surprisingly, the insights deepen the further we are the term and the improvisations become more nuanced.

Entrepreneurs need to listen deeply to their business environment.

Entrepreneurs need to build connected networks.

Entrepreneurs need to put themselves out there even when they are uncomfortable.

Entrepreneurs need to know that their voices matter.

Entrepreneurs need to be improvisational, playful, and responsive.

Entrepreneurs need to be comfortable in liminal spaces.

Entrepreneurs need to apply these same musical skills to brainstorming and creative problem-solving sessions.

All of these insights from a 10-minute collaborative improvisation.

Let me pose the same question to you: what do Deep Listening group-improvisation and entrepreneurship have in common? And what might be possible if we were to apply this practice to other musical or academic settings?

Administrators need to listen deeply to their business environment.

Musicians need to build connected networks.

Scholars need to put themselves out there even when they are uncomfortable.

Students need to know that their voices matter.

Schools of Music need to be improvisational, playful, and responsive.

We all need to be comfortable in liminal spaces.

Entrepreneurs need to apply these same musical skills to brainstorming and creative problem-solving sessions and musicians need to apply these same entrepreneurial skills to inventing a lifetime of artistic moments, one after the next.

What might be possible if every faculty meeting started like this? And every staff meeting? Let's think bigger. What if every Board of Trustees meeting started like this? Why not? After all our goal is to change the entire ecosystem of music education. If we hope to create a culture of creativity, entrepreneurship, collaboration, adaptability, and play then we need to move beyond fear and jump into the sandbox and play.

This creativity culture must go far beyond our students alone. They need role models, mentors, and collaborators. That is why it is so important for professors to join in the collaborations alongside their students.

Think about the possibilities if we were to begin every music theory class in this way. Students and faculty could co-create improvisations based on any mode or scale. Why not musicology? Improvisations would become inspired by musical styles that span the history of our art form. Music educators and experts in improvisation would foster creativity and collaborative skills among our youngest emerging artists and instill a lifetime of joy for music. What if every chamber music rehearsal or studio class started with a guided group improvisation? Pauline Oliveros' Deep Listening pieces open-up treasure troves of guidance and possibilities. (Deep Listening as a superpower deserves a chapter of its own.)

With a bit more work, large ensembles can do this too. The listening must be more subtle and the ability to hold silence more critical. Adjusting directions based on the group size becomes critical. For a group of 20, the goal might be 50% listening and 50% sounding. For a group of 75, the goal might be 75% listening and 25% sounding. Instrumental ensembles can first learn by using their voices alone. And as members become more comfortable with the concepts introduce their instruments as they collectively listen and sound.

The biggest challenge to infusing these practices within ensemble training is overcoming the false belief that group improvisation on this scale can be nothing but chaos. Truthfully, the first attempts will be chaotic. But in those moments, you will need to tap into your own 21st century superpowers, and instead of focusing on all the reasons this can't work, refocus your thinking towards all of the incredible benefits that your students and ensembles will gain when it does work.

Who wouldn't want an ensemble of nuanced super-listeners and creators, eager and willing to add their own musical voice to the mix? And equally willing to hold space for others to do so? This is the type of ensemble the 21st century needs: the creative, entrepreneurial, collaborative, adaptable, playful, empathetic ensemble. And just think about the benefits an ensemble equipped with all these qualities will bring to bear when performing Ludwig van Beethoven, Amy Beach, William Grant Still, or Pauline Oliveros.

Group improvisation is a radically inclusive practice and offers other radical benefits to our institutional ecosystems. It moves us away from simply translating notes on a page and closer to expressing creative ideas shared with others. It becomes about the power of one's own ideas and one's own musical and intellectual contributions blending with other voices in the community. Collaborative improvisation decenters traditional Western Classical music hierarchies, which have historically excluded, discouraged, suppressed, and silenced non-white musicians. Group improvisation offers a space where all musicians can be heard, seen, and valued. A space that lets each participant know that their contributions and ideas matter; that *they* matter.

As music schools strive to build cultures of true belonging, we need to go well beyond expanding repertoire choices, dismantling barriers to entry, and creating a more expansive and inclusive curriculum. We need every person in the community to know that they matter. In this context, collaborative improvisation as a cultural value is next-level equity and inclusion work. Imagine a community where every single member feels that their voice is heard, their voice matters, and their ideas, both musical and intellectual, matter. This kind of personal empowerment builds empowered communities of belonging. Although you might not have thought of collaborative creativity as a path for building systemic equity, systemic diversity, and systemic belonging, what you are likely to discover is that it is foundational for creating a culture supercharged for transformational change.

Building an ecosystem of creativity, entrepreneurship, collaboration, adaptability, and play is a foundational change for most music schools. It will take time and hard work, but the benefits are immeasurable. Not only will students become steeped in the superpowers needed for life after graduation, but it will set the stage for your institution to become The Creative, Entrepreneurial, Collaborative, Adaptable, Playful School of Music we are dreaming about. Radical curricular change becomes so much more feasible when you have a culture of "yes/and," rather than a culture of "but we've always done it that way." This, by the way, is exactly how you actualize thinking outside-of-the-box (a music box, if you will) we've historically trapped ourselves within.

Once equipped with the same superpowers nurtured within our students so that they might enjoy successful careers today and in 2075, our adaptable, flexible, agile music schools can focus their creative collaborations on curricular change, new majors, and degree programs. This does not mean that institutions should be in a constant state of reinvention. Rather schools can now ask themselves if they are truly preparing their graduates for fulfilling musical lives and if not, have the confidence to make timely changes as needed. This type of school is built to handle change. Even unexpected changes, like a pandemic.

Even more exciting, this school is built to drive change. What?! A music school can be the change leader in our field? Why not? This is where entrepreneurial thinking kicks in, and your creativity culture can brainstorm and jam and play its way towards redefining performance, distribution, engagement, community impact, education, production, composition, and other areas not yet imagined. This is exciting stuff. This is the buzz of creative possibility felt emanating from every hallway. Who wouldn't want to be a part of a community of infinite potential? I know I would. And I imagine you would too.

These are exciting times. We have a mandate and an opportunity to reimagine how we train our future musicians. In order to give our graduates the superpowers of creativity, entrepreneurship, collaboration, adaptability, and playfulness, we all have to—we all get to—roll these superpowers into our own musical lives and into the DNA of our institutional identities. This needs to happen because the world needs our music, our magic, and our transformational medicine more than ever.

As we make these changes in our music programs, let's then take collaborative creativity to the next level and infuse these practices into our national music school ecosystem. Let's bring our institutions themselves together to join in a meta-ensemble of collaborative improvisation and play—musical play, entrepreneurial play, and turn-dreams-into-reality play. I am smiling just thinking about it and hope to see you soon and at the next College Music Society collaborative improv meta-jam!

For Further Reading

Ackerman, Diane. *Deep Play*. New York: Vintage Books 1999.
Nachmanovitch, Stephen. *Free Play: Improvisation in Life and Art*. Los Angeles: J.P. Tarcher, Inc. 1990.
Nachmanovitch, Stephen. *The Art of Is.* Novato: New World Library 2019.
Oliveros, Pauline. *Deep Listening: A Composer's Sound Practice*. Kingston: Deep Listening Publications 2005.
Sarath, Edward W.; Myers, David E.; Campbell, Patricia, Campbell Shehan. *Redefining Music Studies in an Age of Change: Creativity, Diversity, and Integration*. 1st ed. New York: Routledge 2017.

4 Readying Our Classical Music Performers – An Employer's View

Kendra Whitlock Ingram

Introduction

Making a living as a musician often means choreographing and coordinating a diverse mix of potential revenue streams. This requires creativity, networking, marketing, and a host of skills that have nothing to do with playing a musical instrument. Focused on employability as a key outcome, faculty and administrators must evolve music school curricula to include programmatic and pre-professional experiences that embrace the non-performance skills required if they are to prepare musicians to thrive in the contemporary musical landscape.

Throughout this chapter, the topic of musician employability will be explored through three lenses:
The Employment Landscape for Professional Musicians

> Anchoring upon employment and survey data, Section One provides a statistical snapshot of today's musician employment prospects and captures how professional musicians feel about various aspects of their professional life.

Reflections of Industry Experts

> Drawing upon insights culled from seasoned music industry employers, Section Two reflects upon the attributes of highly employable musicians and offers music faculty and administrators key takeaways and recommendations for curricular transformation.

How a Global Pandemic and American Racial Reckoning Will Affect Future Generations of Professional Musicians

DOI: 10.4324/9781003218630-4

Readying Our Classical Music Performers – An Employer's View

Acknowledging the impact of a global pandemic and the racial reckoning of 2020, music faculty and administrators can no longer afford to dismiss the societal and economic pressures music graduates carry with them as they enter into an uncertain profession and world. Section Three reflects upon stark statistical data about what professional musicians experience "on the job."

Preparing music students for all aspects of professional life (economic, emotional, and social) must become embedded within the curriculum and music school experience if we are to prepare music students for the careers that await them.

Section One: The Employment Landscape for Professional Musicians

The Musician's Post-Graduation Path to Employment

As students consider college degree programs, post-graduation employability is too often seen as important but far too distant into the future. Students see college degree programs – defined by one's cumulative knowledge, skills, and experiences – as the beginning of a journey of exploration and learning that eventually leads to "getting that diploma." The challenge, however, in today's competitive performing arts workplace is that students need to consider this "far off" goal much earlier in their career-mapping journey.

As music faculty and administrators, we must ask ourselves fundamental questions about our obligations for preparing music students for life after graduation, including what kinds of jobs remain available to music performers post-graduation? And how can we help our graduates achieve career sustainability, wealth-building prospects, and artistic fulfillment? To greater or lesser extents, all degree programs grapple with these questions as they send graduates into the post-academic world. Music performance degree programs' challenge (and perhaps performing arts in general) is to find curricular solutions for balancing growth in "art-making" and skill-building in the business of the arts.

While conducting interviews for this chapter, I reflected upon my own experience as a music school graduate. I remember the fear of looking out onto the employment horizon for performers and taking note of the limited ways of making a livable wage. For classical musicians, the coveted full-time position in a professional orchestra was widely seen as the ultimate post-graduation job. Guaranteeing a full-time salary, health and retirement benefits, and maybe even a bit of artistic fulfillment, the full-time orchestral musician could enjoy consistent and stable employment across an entire career. In some cases, salary and benefits afforded the opportunity to build wealth through home ownership, retirement savings, and the gift of a relatively flexible schedule that made possible additional revenue-generating opportunities such as lucrative teaching positions and additional paid performances. These full-time gigs, however, proved highly competitive.

Many professional musicians have built careers performing as freelance artists. The spectrum of employability as a freelance musician is vast and ranges from a major solo career to sporadic paid performances. One of the challenges facing newly minted music graduates is understanding exactly what falls on this employment spectrum and how to navigate the opportunities presented.

Too frequently, music graduates only seek employment opportunities that have become familiar to them during their academic careers. Typically, these include two options of "playing a gig" for pay: 1) a formal performance with an audience (including concerts and church gigs), or 2) background music for an event (like a wedding or party).

So, the question becomes: how might we expand our graduates' vision of what professional musicians do to make a life and make a living?

Employment versus Underemployment

Throughout my 24-years as a full-time performing arts industry professional, I've been acutely aware of the concept of underemployment among musicians. Underemployment measures labor force utilization of skills, experience, and availability to work within the economy.[1] People classified as underemployed include highly skilled workers working in low-paying and/or low-skilled jobs or those working part-time who are seeking full-time employment. Among most music performance graduates underemployment proves to be a greater threat than unemployment.

Two recent studies conducted by the National Endowment for the Arts (NEA) and the Music Industry Research Association (MIRA) provide interesting data about the employability of professional musicians.

In 2019, the NEA published "Artists and Other Cultural Workers: a Statistical Report." This research focused on those whose primary or secondary jobs are as artists. These individuals represent both salary-and-wage and self-employed earners, the latter of whom, for the purposes of this chapter, will be referred to as freelance musicians. The refers to the former – those for whom being an artist is a secondary job – as "moonlighting artists." "Moonlighting artists" meet our definition of underemployed musicians. The report states that:

> In 2017, a total of 288,000 workers were employed as musicians. 188,000 musicians consider "musician" their primary occupation (the job at which the individual worked the greatest number of hours). That same year, an estimated 100,000 workers held second jobs as musicians, making up 34.8 percent of the total number of working musicians."

The NEA report also examined data from a 2018 survey jointly conducted by the Music Industry Research Association (MIRA) and the Princeton University Survey Research Center. Designed to "study the life circumstances and well-being of professional musicians and composers,"[2] the survey included approximately 1,200 individuals earning a living as a musician or composer or endeavoring to do so. Three interesting data points were outlined regarding salary and income:

- The median musician surveyed reported an annual salary of $35,000.
- 61 percent of musicians said that their music-related income was not sufficient to meet their living expenses.
- Seventy percent cited "financial insecurity" as what they least liked about being a professional musician.

These data reveal some good news and bad news: music performance graduates have a good chance of working full-time as a musician post-graduation, but the outlook on their earning potential is not as positive. These data are not shared to paint a grim picture of the music profession, but to illuminate the challenges and realities facing professional musicians: something we must consider as we prepare music graduates for the working world.

Today's Employers: Who are They? Who are They Hiring? And why?

What may surprise many about the inner workings of the nonprofit and commercial music industries, is that many of the individuals making career decisions on behalf of artists are neither accomplished nor formally trained musicians themselves. Many presenters who oversee multi-disciplinary programming have backgrounds in other performing arts disciplines. And in some cases, are trained in completely different fields of study, with little or no background in the arts at all.

The exception to this rule tends to be among large producing performing arts organizations (e.g., symphony orchestras, opera companies, dance companies), for which the level of expertise required to curate and produce programming is both specialized and requires advanced knowledge about the art form. Within these organizations, artistic staff (e.g., directors, conductors, choreographers) become directly involved in hiring decisions. These organizations, however, make up a small percentage of the "hiring ecosystem" for musicians, particularly when considering freelance musician employment opportunities.

So, who are the individuals making hiring decisions for freelance musicians? The list is expansive and consists of a diverse mix of marketing directors, wedding planners, church staff, advertising agencies, restaurant and club owners, and more, all of whom have varying needs and expectations. Do these needs and expectations rise to the scrutiny experienced during an undergraduate jury? Probably not. So, if improving employment outcomes for music performance graduates is the goal, then helping students understand who is overseeing the hiring process and what their needs and expectations are becoming important learning outcomes within pre-professional training.

For more than two decades, I've contracted headliners to perform for thousands of people and hired freelance musicians to play for small private events. Invariably when negotiating business dealings with colleagues within the music industry ecosystem – managers, agents, and other "talent buyers" – this question arises: Who we are hiring and why? Frequently – during what was otherwise meant to be a logistical conversation – a philosophical discussion emerges about how academia can better prepare the next generation of music industry artists.

Experts interviewed for this chapter outlined some basic "must-haves" for hiring musicians. Dan Israel articulated this so well: "I expect players I hire to be prepared and on time. The musician should want to make things very easy for the person who is hiring them, which means they should also be easy to work with, friendly, and organized. The musicians should be able to communicate clearly in writing and on phone."[3] Throughout several of my interviews with experts within the field, I heard feedback that employers wanted to hire people who are kind and respectful of others, both to performers on stage and the people behind the scenes. The assumption here is that technical ability and musicianship are certainly factors in hiring, but these additional criteria are nearly as important, as well.

Readying Our Classical Music Performers – An Employer's View 91

Section Two: Reflections of Industry Experts

Drawing upon insights from experts in the field, this section aims to reposition the reader's perspective towards that of the employer's point-of-view. By doing so, the hope is to offer music faculty key insights and actionable takeaways that can be used strategically to transform and strengthen music performance programs in higher education: insights and takeaways that aim to improve employment outcomes for graduating music performers.

The primary selection criteria for vetting interviewees for this chapter included: 1) expertise in the music industry field; 2) music graduates of institutions of higher education, albeit across multiple generations;[4] (See Table 4.1); 3) extensive experience with the Western European classical music tradition, and 4) expertise working across multiple genres. Additionally, each expert has a direct connection – either personally or as an employer – with musicians trained in a traditional conservatory model.[5] Despite this criterion, it is important to note that each expert comes to this work with diverse perspectives.

A 4-year college degree has value beyond improving employment outcomes (of course). It is, however, the collective perspective of the industry experts interviewed for this chapter that employability has been neglected as a key outcome and that musicians' education must become a more equitable balance of artistic fulfillment, post-graduation employability, wealth attainment, and financial security, and sustainable wellness. And that when this is accomplished, we will see a reduction in underemployment, industry flight, burnout, an increase in wage earnings, and full-time employment.

Table 4.1 Music Industry Experts Interviewed

Chris Harrington, Senior Director of Jazz and @theMax, Detroit Symphony Orchestra (current); President and CEO, Ordway Performing Arts Center (effective November 1, 2021)

Dan Israel, Assistant Director of Touring, Jazz at Lincoln Center

Rika Iino, Founder/Producer, Sozo Artists

Lee Prinz, President, and CEO, Colbert Artists Management

Camille Delaney-McNeil, Musician and Director, Beckmen YOLA Center, Los Angeles Philharmonic

Britney Coleman, Working Musical Theatre Professional

Dan Haskins, Working Professional Percussionist, and Orchestra Contractor

Over multiple hours of interviews, three common themes emerged that prove useful when reimagining how we might prepare more employable music school graduates:

1 Connection and Collaboration: developing Musicians Who Can Engage and Collaborate
2 Greater Emphasis on Professional Development and Employment Skill-Building
3 Holistic Education with an Emphasis on Developing a Well-Rounded Music School Graduate

Theme 1 – Connection and Collaboration: Developing Musicians Who Can Engage and Collaborate

The importance of a musician's ability to successfully connect with audiences and collaborate with others was expressed by nearly every expert interviewed. The experts, uniformly and unprompted, emphasized audience engagement and collaboration as critically important. They too noted a remarked deficiency of these skills among classical musicians. Some readers may say, "But we're in the business of connecting with people through music." Nonetheless, connecting with audiences and collaborating with other artists and professionals are specific skill sets that must be fostered within music training and are too frequently neglected. Many of the experts observed how little academic focus is placed on developing musicians' proficiency in connecting and collaborating and that this was true across all instruments offered within music performance degree programs.

Rika Iino reflected on the Maya Angelou quote, "I've learned that people will forget what you said, people will forget what you did, but people will never forget how you made them feel."[6] When considering signing an artist to her roster, Iino said she looks for someone who is "bold enough to take risks for themselves, has a collaborative nature, and cares about making a social impact on the world through their art."[7] This is a tall order. Lee Prinz referenced similar criteria for signing artists at Colbert Artists: "You need an artist who has something unique to say." Prinz reflected, "A musician needs to be relatable and if you're not, you have to be just so supremely talented. You have to find connectability, beyond just being technically excellent. They were not talking about this concept of connection when we were in school."[8]

Thinking about the ways in which we assess our undergraduate music students, the concept of the semester-end "jury" comes to mind. Numerous examples of music school jury grading rubrics can be found on websites across the internet. Nearly all rubrics assess qualities such as tone, intonation, articulation, technical facility, dynamic expressions, and phrasing. Virtually none of the rubrics include assessments on communication skills, audience engagement, or – interestingly – creativity.

The educational assessment of excellence among music students has long focused on technical skills. Experts, however, would argue that employability requires skill development in what is often referred to as "stage presence." And stage presence today means so much more than a polished look and acknowledgment of one's accompanist.

Although experts did not contest that proficiency in one's instrument remains essential, Iino raised the concern: "How do you create innovation within the rigors of a classical music setting? It's not easy."[9] Chris Harrington spoke at length about how he often attends performances of musicians he wants to hire, with the explicit goal of assessing how they connect with audiences. "When I go to shows, I'm generally familiar with an artist musically. When considering an artist, I'd like to hire for my programming, I'm really attending to watch the audiences and how they are responding."[10] He described how he likes to sit in different locations throughout the hall so that he can observe audience engagement: a significant factor in influencing his decision. He also wants to see how the artist is engaging with their fellow musicians.

Key Takeaways and Recommendations:

- Restructure milestone recitals and the semester-end jury to allow for more student-driven construction of the program. Consider expanding the grading rubric to assess connection with audiences, creative programming, innovation, and perhaps entertainment value.
- Invite non-experts (a typical audience member, a community member, non-musicians) into the evaluation process. Other performing arts disciplines – like dance for example – have this element built into student jury evaluation processes. Ask: what are the best practices we can adopt from other disciplines?
- Assign a collaboration component for every recital or jury, requiring students to engage colleagues across genres or subject areas outside of the music discipline [e.g., the business school, "group project" grading style][11]
- Incorporate regular collaborative practices throughout the academic career; skill-building through persuasion, negotiating, and conflict resolution.

Theme 2 – Emphasis on Professional Development and Employment Skill-Building

Starkly revealing were the experts' consistent recommendations for a greater emphasis on professional development and employment skill-building within the music school curriculum. Below are some of the recommendations made for developing musicians with diverse skills for the current (and future) music industry ecosystem.

Echoing earlier concerns about music schools' narrow focus on technical proficiency on a single instrument, some experts questioned if music programs (via studio teachers) are building the "right" type of technical proficiency. Or if there are alternative approaches to technical proficiency that would better serve students' success when entering the professional world.

Often, students choose the school they attend based on the studio teacher with whom they will study. As Dan Israel put it, "Students and parents are making major life decisions [deciding on a college] based on an individual teacher."[12] Understanding that the private studio teacher plays an influential role in a music student's academic program, Dan Haskins argued that the studio teacher can unilaterally direct where a student's technical skill-building will be focused. Wearing his "orchestra contractor" and "Broadway pit musician" hats, Haskins reflected, "Students are learning solo repertoire as a primary part of their applied studies, but not consistently studying major orchestral excerpt work. A number of my professional orchestra musician colleagues and I discussed that students spend a lot of time learning virtuosic solo repertoire, but these pieces have nothing to do with being a working professional in an orchestra. They're learning a skill that helps them to get a doctorate."[13] As an employer, Haskins frequently looks for musicians who can blend and are adept within their role as an ensemble member (rather than seeing themselves as soloists) for any given "gig."

Expressing concerns that the culture of the "studio" is often hierarchical, the experts noted that a studio ethos of teachers "imparting wisdom" and students "taking direction" is inherently problematic. Studio teachers too often have rigid (or even formulaic) expectations of how the instruments should be played and what repertoire should be studied. Recommending a pivot toward a more collaborative studio teacher-student partnership, the experts envision students' academic experiences as collaborative journeys that empower students to make artistic choices earlier in their academic careers and build skills through integrated professional and artistic experiences. As Camille

Delaney-McNeil said, perhaps the studio teacher could take on the role of "shepherding young learners to find their authentic and unique artistic voice," rather than creating a failed legacy of creating copycats of the studio teacher.[14]

Delaney-Smith eloquently outlined what she feels should be the overarching goal of any music performance degree program: "To produce the highest quality artist who can 1) authentically represent themselves and find their artistic voice, however that manifests, and 2) celebrate and encourage all paths within the music school ecosystem without judgment."[15]

Listening to Delaney-Smith's perspective on this, I am immediately reminded of *The Frost Method®*, a curriculum formula branded by the Frost School of Music at the University of Miami. It clearly and succinctly outlines the goals for its students:

> *The Frost Method® integrates the values and skills below into the Frost School's curriculum to help you succeed in the rapidly changing world of professional music.*
>
> *At Frost, there are no barriers between disciplines. Students have the opportunity to perform and learn across departments and genres.*
>
> *The Frost Method® will help you become more than an external musician who reads music and interprets, but also an internal musician who understands and creates music from the inside out." Dean Shelly Berg.*[16]

Although Frost's employment statistics (outlined below) may not differ dramatically from other music school programs, it does make great sense that The Frost School markets its student employment outcomes prominently on its website.

> *With the groundbreaking Frost Method® curriculum, students build themselves into musicians with artistic, technological, and entrepreneurial skills to thrive in the 21st century. 91.3% of Frost graduates find a full-time job, or go to graduate school, within six months of graduation!*[17]

What is revealing and consistent between Delaney-Smith's stated goal and that of *The Frost Method®*, is that neither mentions technical proficiency. Both, however, reference "no barriers" and "learning across disciplines." Nonetheless, most music schools today continue to preserve a conservatory model that often contradicts these goals and potentially stifles program innovation needed to advance student development.

Across all interviews, frequent references were made to the decreasing relevance music schools have for preparing students for the 21st century music industry marketplace. More specifically, ignoring the diverse tastes, trends, and interests of 21st century audiences (and artists) in favor of a relentless emphasis on the Western European classical music canon and the misalignment of these decisions with graduates' employment opportunities.

Even when considering the nimbler path often afforded to musical theatre majors, rigidity persists as evidenced in schools' commitment to preparing a "certain type" of Broadway performer. Employability outcomes for graduates of musical theatre programs are most often centered around "booking a Broadway show" as a marker of career success. Much like their classical counterparts who center on the full-time orchestral job as the ideal success outcome, musical theatre programs train students to achieve, as Britney Coleman outlined, "a typical Broadway mold that [was once] commercially viable."[18] But does this framework any longer fit within the constantly evolving music industry marketplace? And mightn't students benefit from a broader approach to musical theatre training?

Although the concept of a "triple threat" artist (one who could sing, dance, and act equally well) increases employability, one can also argue that a vocalist equipped to perform proficiently in diverse styles holds equal value. Broadway superstar Kelli O'Hara can act and dance well, but her true superpower is her ability to sing exceptionally well in classical and contemporary styles. In a 2017 *American Theatre Magazine* article – authored by Oklahoma City University Director of Opera and Musical Theater and former O'Hara voice professor – David Herendeen references O'Hara when stating, "We know we have to prepare our students to be nimble and adapt to whatever the current market is. Kelli [O'Hara] is a really good example of somebody that paid attention to the industry and what it was demanding."[19]

Artistic agility and proficiency in various styles or genres of music (never mind another instrument) enhances music school graduates' employability. For most traditional music performance degree programs, however, students are required to focus on primarily one instrument and one genre of music, with very little room for exploration.

Haskins, reflecting on his own experience as a student of the conservatory model and how he might have benefited from exploring diverse styles of music as part of his education (particularly through his interest as a percussionist), said "Part of the college experience should be to learn music that doesn't translate to your specific major directly." He noted that there is great value in a "well-rounded music education and just the joy of playing music and learning something outside of what you typically do."[20]

Delaney-McNeil noted that students need to arrive at graduation "with an ability to navigate the world as a musician."[21] Echoed by all experts interviewed was the need for music graduates to acquire fundamental skills in the business of the arts, including an understanding of contract negotiations, basic tax preparation as a Schedule C Form 1040 self-employed musician, and how to access resources for musician benefits and services.

Prinz, Haskins, and Iino pressed further, suggesting that musicians must learn how to leverage social media to sell their brand and that this begins by gaining a comprehensive understanding of what goes into establishing a brand as an artist. Haskins made an interesting point about how he has hired players strictly based on viewing their YouTube Channel or TikTok accounts. "You have to have a major presence on social media. The days of getting a gig via a resume are gone."[22]

Networking also plays an important role in building a career. Haskins stated, "students out of school often move to a major market like New York to find more work, but they don't always make the connection that networking both in-person and through social media leads to more work."[23]

Key Takeaways and Recommendations:

- Broaden skillsets required in the assessment of recital/jury model: placing less weight on mastering virtuosic solo repertoire, and a greater focus on audition skills, ensemble playing, proficiency in diverse styles, and perhaps improvisation.
- Place greater emphasis on how to build a personal brand and develop a marketing strategy to promote oneself as a professional musician. Require students to develop a "digital promotion portfolio" as part of the required student outcomes for graduation.
- Integrate "musician life skills" into the curriculum.
- Add a graduation requirement of one non-performance internship for all music majors to build industry context.[24]
- Embrace a "mutual learning exchange" model that encourages studio teachers to guide, rather than dictate students' journeys of developing their own voices as an artist.[25]
- Encourage students to develop an intentional process for professional mentorship throughout the academic program.

Theme 3 – Holistic Education with An Emphasis on Developing a Well-Rounded Music School Graduate

The experts repeatedly commented on the correlation between becoming a well-rounded person and being a successful working musician. This concept was related by some experts as being a well-rounded musician (as discussed earlier in Theme 2), but the common through line was an emphasis on developing musicians who are good citizens of the world. From the agent/manager perspective, Prinz and Iino both commented on how they were most interested in working with artists who care about the community and giving back. Iino highlighted that one thing all of her artists have in common is that "they look to the world outside of their own discipline for everything from inspiration to revenue-generating opportunities. They also consider the societal impact of their artistic work."[26]

Harrington and Israel had similar thoughts about basic professional qualities, including the importance of "being kind and respecting other people's time." "This business is so small and these qualities matter when making a decision between hiring two artists," Harrington reflected.[27] Delaney-McNeil went further to consider artists as "leaders of our generation" who are "obsessive about evolving" in order to meet the changing times.

If the professional working musician's role extends beyond simply being an artistically inspiring performer and includes an obligation for being a "good citizen" and "leader for our generation," then students must understand how their work intersects with and impacts the world around them. This is an exciting prospect for higher education music programs: imagine the limitless possibilities at the intersection of music and every academic field of study.

The experts also reflected extensively on how a more intentional process for professional mentorship could help broaden students' perspectives throughout their academic journey. This mentorship should happen in partnership with academic advisors and faculty, essentially seeding a professional network for the soon-to-be professional working musician.

Key Takeaways and Recommendations:

- Provide regular opportunities (throughout the academic program) for students to engage with expansive "thinkers and doers" from inside and outside the music industry.
- Integrate cross-curricular connections outside the music school.
- Incentivize music students to incorporate cross-curricular collaborations in their class projects, performances, recitals, and beyond.

Readying Our Classical Music Performers – An Employer's View 99

Section Three: How a Global Pandemic and American Racial Reckoning Will Affect Future Generations of Professional Musicians

After shutting down nearly every aspect of the live performing arts industry for nearly 18-months, it is difficult to ponder the prospects of future graduates without reflecting on the pandemic's impact on performing musicians. A Pittsburgh Post-Gazette article from July 2021 reported on how some professional freelance musicians were either "adjusting their careers to include more stable side hustles in the aftermath of the pandemic" or "hanging up their instruments for good."[28] How music programs account for the difficult lessons learned at this moment remains to be realized.

The murder of George Floyd in May 2020 sparked a racial reckoning that has rippled throughout every facet of American life and industry. The performing arts across all disciplines had to come to terms with its own systemic racism and how change can be affected within white-dominated, Western European classical traditions.[29] Developing professional musicians possessing cultural competencies will be an essential element in navigating the employment marketplace. Employers will demand it.[30]

Even prior to the global pandemic and racial reckoning of 2020, professional musicians have endured social and emotional issues connected to the nature of their work. Revisiting key findings from the *2018 Music Industry Research Association (MIRA) Survey of Musicians* illuminates issues and concerns music school graduates may (or will likely) encounter as they search for post-graduation employment:

- 61 percent of musicians said their music-related income was not sufficient to cover living expenses.
- Women, representing roughly one-third of working musicians, reported experiencing high rates of discrimination and sexual harassment.
- 63 percent of non-white musicians said they faced racial discrimination, as compared to 36 percent of non-white, self-employed workers nationwide.
- 50 percent of musicians reported struggling with issues involving mental health.
- Incidence of substance abuse was substantially higher among musicians than in the general public.

The statistics outlined above illuminate the fact that professional musicians are experiencing social/emotional workplace challenges at alarming rates. As we work to prepare our students for a fulfilling, sustainable career in music performance, we must too find ways to prepare them for the realities facing musicians today. Britney Coleman, who has been consistently and successfully working as a musical theatre artist since she graduated from the University of Michigan in 2011, says she was not prepared for the mental and physical fatigue of performing eight shows per week for weeks or even months at a stretch: "That is the reality of the job that they just don't prepare you for in school. It's never going to be like it is in school with just a weekend of shows. I had to figure out how to build endurance and take care of myself both physically and mentally."[31]

Although academic models could never, nor should they hope to, mimic an actual working job, we must find ways to simulate aspects of professional work within our academic frameworks. Coleman mentioned how summer stock theatre work was her first glimpse into the rigors of a regular performing schedule. She also talked about receiving encouragement from faculty and advisors to take some of the summer to rest and recharge.

How might we institutionalize discussions that help students strike a balance between gaining invaluable "real world" experiences and taking time to recharge when considering summer opportunities?

Key Takeaways and Recommendations:

- Incorporate curricular opportunities for students to develop a personal "toolkit" for self-care, wellness, and resiliency.
- Engage students in conversation about MIRA study findings shared above.
- Encourage/require students to experience pre-professional work for at least one summer during their academic program.

Final Reflection

In my interviews about improving employment outcomes for music school graduates, the experts recognized the complexities of change management within music higher education. Nonetheless, some are worried that the most daunting obstacle to meeting the changing demands of the music industry marketplace is embedded within music schools' propensity to "preserve tradition" rather than reward innovation. My worry is that music in higher education's commitment to resist change will prove to be the source of its own demise.

I deeply believe that if we start teaching the "hustle skills" in our music programs, we will develop graduates who have both a strong understanding of the industry and the know-how to navigate and thrive within it.

Rika Iino asked a question I continue to ponder: "How do we create innovation within the rigors of a classical music setting?"[32] We know it's possible because we see examples modeled for us.

One of the world's most respected and beloved classical musicians, Yo-Yo Ma continues to push his own musical boundaries by collaborating with musicians of diverse genres, artists in other disciplines, and individuals in non-artistic fields. Pre-pandemic, Ma built a tour performing the Bach Cello Suites in cities around the world, pairing each performance with a "Day of Action." Connecting with communities and stimulating discussions about social justice issues,[33] Ma demonstrates what it can mean to serve as an inspiration as a musician and as a human being, how we can continually reach broader audiences, stay relevant in changing times, and remain employed.

Students graduating from music performance programs will face challenges in building sustainable and fulfilling performance careers. To thrive, graduates of today and the near future will also have more opportunities to define their one-of-a-kind paths. Our obligation is to ensure that they have all of the skills to take advantage of those opportunities.

Notes

1. See the definition of underemployment here: https://www.investopedia.com/terms/u/underemployment.asp
2. Home page for MIRA survey information; introduction statement: https://psrc.princeton.edu/news/mira-survey-musicians-april-june-2018
3. Dan Israel, interview with Kendra Whitlock Ingram, July 19, 2021, transcript
4. The interview format included questions tailored to presenters, agents/managers, and working musicians. In some cases, there was overlap, depending on the experts' professional experiences. All interviews were recorded via Zoom audio with supplemental interview questionnaire form notes.
5. My colleagues are graduates of music programs at Eastman, University of Rochester, Wayne State University, University of Michigan, Peabody Institute, Manhattan School of Music, and Columbia University.
6. Maya Angelou's quote
7. Rika Iino, interview with Kendra Whitlock Ingram, July 19, 2021, and July 26, 2021, transcript.
8. Lee Prinz, interview with Kendra Whitlock Ingram, July 24, 2021, transcript.
9. Rika Iino, interview with Kendra Whitlock Ingram, July 19, 2021, and July 26, 2021, transcript.

10 Chris Harrington, interview with Kendra Whitlock Ingram, July 20, 2021, and July 25, 2021, transcript.
11 Idea from Rika Iino, interview with Kendra Whitlock Ingram, July 19, 2021, and July 26, 2021, transcript.
12 Dan Israel, interview with Kendra Whitlock Ingram, July 19, 2021, transcript
13 Dan Haskins, interview with Kendra Whitlock Ingram, July 31, 2021, transcript.
14 Camille Delaney-McNeil, interview with Kendra Whitlock Ingram, July 20, 2021, and July 25, 2021, transcript.
15 Camille Delaney-McNeil, interview with Kendra Whitlock Ingram, July 20, 2021, and July 25, 2021, transcript.
16 The branding and simplicity of The Frost Method is really a model for other schools.
17 Again, one of the few schools that highlight employment outcomes prominently on their website. Longy School of Music at Bard also has a compelling home page that is student-centered: https://longy.edu/
18 Britney Coleman, interview with Kendra Whitlock Ingram, July 28, 2021, transcript.
19 It should be noted that Kelli O'Hara is equally excellent in opera and musical theatre performance and that Oklahoma City University prides itself on equally valuing both genres as part of the vocal program. Gilroy, M. "Musical Theatre Students Are Becoming Quadruple Threats." American Theatre Magazine, January 2017
20 Dan Haskins, interview with Kendra Whitlock Ingram, July 31, 2021, transcript.
21 Camille Delaney-McNeil, interview with Kendra Whitlock Ingram, July 20, 2021, and July 25, 2021, transcript.
22 Dan Haskins, interview with Kendra Whitlock Ingram, July 31, 2021, transcript.
23 Dan Haskins, interview with Kendra Whitlock Ingram, July 31, 2021, transcript.
24 Dan Israel and Chris Harrington both suggested this idea. Camille Delaney-McNeil referenced her personal experience working as an intern in human resources for the McDonald's Corporation and how that gave her such a better sense of how to manage people, collaborate, and understand the complexities of people management.
25 Camille Delaney-McNeil, interview with Kendra Whitlock Ingram, July 20, 2021, and July 25, 2021, transcript.
26 Rika Iino, interview with Kendra Whitlock Ingram, July 19, 2021, and July 26, 2021, transcript.
27 Chris Harrington, interview with Kendra Whitlock Ingram, July 20, 2021, and July 25, 2021, transcript.
28 See Reynolds, J. "Freelance musicians found new passions during the pandemic. Some aren't going back." *Pittsburgh Post-Gazette*, July 22, 2021. Accessed July 22, 2021. https://www.post-gazette.com/ae/music/2021/07/22/Independent-musicians-career-changes-pandemic-Pittsburgh-2021/stories/202107140136. This is one of many articles during the pandemic year about musicians and the existential crisis they face about giving up music in order to make a living. Professional musicians

have always struggled with this, but the pandemic has definitely given more artists pause about having to weather future business interruptions.
29 Again, numerous articles since June 2020 about systemic racism within the Western European art forms, but this one from the Washington Post relates well to the need for change in the Conservatory model. See Brodeur, M.A. "That Sound You're Hearing Is Classical Music's Long Overdue Reckoning With Racism." Washington Post, July 16, 2020, accessed August 1, 2021. https://www.washingtonpost.com/lifestyle/style/that-sound-youre-hearing-is-classical-musics-long-overdue-reckoning-with-racism/2020/07/15/1b883e76-c49c-11ea-b037-f9711f89ee46_story.html. I am quoted in this article from last summer which outlines how commercial theatre is experiencing a similar reckoning and responding. See: Paulson, M. "At Theaters, Push for Racial Equity Leads to Resignations and Restructuring." *NY Times*, August 19, 2020. Accessed on July 31, 2021. https://www.nytimes.com/2020/08/19/theater/racial-equity-theater-resignations.html
30 The Association for Performing Arts Professional announced a pledge to advance racial equity, diversity, and inclusion in arts organizations nationwide. See their website to learn more and to see who has signed the pledge so far: https://www.apap365.org/Programs/10-20-30
31 Britney Coleman, interview with Kendra Whitlock Ingram, July 28, 2021, transcript.
32 Rika Iino, interview with Kendra Whitlock Ingram, July 19, 2021, and July 26, 2021, transcript.
33 I was in Denver in 2019 when Ma performed to thousands at Red Rocks Amphitheatre and led a "Day of Action." This article speaks in-depth about the project: "Why Yo-Yo Ma thinks culture and music can help protect the planet." National Geographic Magazine, May 2021.

Bibliography

2018 Inaugural Music Industry Research Association (MIRA) Survey of Musicians. Report. Music Industry Research and Association (MIRA) Princeton Survey Research Center. Princeton, NJ: MIRA, 2018. Accessed July 15, 2021. https://psrc.princeton.edu/news/mira-survey-musicians-april-june-2018

A Decade of Arts Engagement: Findings from the Survey of Public Participation in the Arts, 2002–2012. Report No. 58. National Endowment for the Arts. Washington, DC: National Endowment for the Arts, 2019. Accessed on July 16, 2021. https://www.arts.gov/sites/default/files/2012-sppa-feb2015.pdf

Artists and Other Cultural Workers A Statistical Portrait. Report. National Endowment for the Arts. Washington, DC: National Endowment for the Arts, 2015. Accessed on July 12, 2021, https://www.arts.gov/sites/default/files/Artists_and_Other_Cultural_Workers.pdf

"Frost School of Music, University of Miami." *Frost School of Music, University of Miami*. Accessed July 30, 2021. http://languages.oberlin.edu/blogs/ctie/tag/curriculum/.https://www.frost.miami.edu/about-us/uniquely-frost/the-frost-method/index.html

Gilroy, M. "Musical Theatre Students Are Becoming Quadruple Threats." American Theatre Magazine, January 2017, Accessed July 23, 2021. https://www.americantheatre.org/2017/01/04/musical-theatre-students-are-becoming-quadruple-threats/

Kalb, C. "Why Yo-Yo Ma thinks culture and music can help protect the planet." National Geographic Magazine, May 2021. Accessed September 11, 2021. https://www.nationalgeographic.co.uk/environment-and-conservation/2021/04/why-yo-yo-ma-thinks-culture-and-music-can-help-protect-the

Kerr, E. and Wood S. "See 10 Years Of Average Student Loan Debt." U.S. News. September 14, 2021. Accessed December 6, 2021. https://www.usnews.com/education/best-colleges/paying-for-college/articles/see-how-student-loan-borrowing-has-risen-in-10-years

Paulson, M. *"At Theaters, Push for Racial Equity Leads to Resignations and Restructuring."* NY Times, August 19, 2020. Accessed on July 31, 2021. https://www.nytimes.com/2020/08/19/theater/racial-equity-theater-resignations.html

Reynolds, J. "Freelance musicians found new passions during the pandemic. Some aren't going back." *Pittsburgh Post-Gazette*, July 22, 2021. Accessed July 22, 2021. https://www.post-gazette.com/ae/music/2021/07/22/Independent-musicians-career-changes-pandemic-Pittsburgh-2021/stories/202107140136

Index

Note: *Italicized* and **bold** page numbers refer to figures and tables, respectively. Page numbers followed by "n" refer to notes.

adaptability 70–72
American racial reckoning, effect on future generations of professional musicians 99–100
amplification 26–28
Angelou, M. 92
Apple 8
arena, establishment of 16–18
"Artists and Other Cultural Workers: a Statistical Report" (NEA) 88
assessments 31–32
Association for Performing Arts Professional 103n30
assumption stomping 22–23
Attitudes 28–29
authentic performance practice 8

Black Lives Matter movement 64, 73, 74
book club 32
bottom-up leadership 12–13
Brown, B. 40
budget 6, 69

Carolina/College Music Society Summit 2.0 2, 19; Curriculum Gameboard *20*
Caruso, D. R. 47
CECAP School of Music 75
Challenge 14–15
change management 100

Coleman, B. 96, 100
collaboration 67–68, 82, 92–93
collaborative improvisation 67, 68, 84
communication: interpersonal 46, 48, 49; proactive 5
community 55; attributes of, and heart/mind work 51–53; concerts 24; conversation 24; engagement 5, 10
compassion 42, 47
connection 51, 92–93
Constraints 15
creative problem-solving 8
creativity 8, 66–68, 77–81, 83
Criteria 15, 16
cross-pollination 9
culture statement 28–29
curricula 6; DEIB in 56–58

Deep Listening 44, 79, 82, 83
DEIB (diversity, equity, inclusion, and belonging) 39–41, 46; in curricula and classroom environments 56–58
Delaney-McNeil, C. 94–95, 97, 98, 102n24
Delaney-Smith, C. 95
Dempster, S. 71
diversity 38–39

EDI (equity, diversity, and inclusion) 5
ego, defeating 49–51

Eilish, B. 63
EI *see* emotional intelligence
elitism 64
emotional intelligence (EI): strategies in heart and mind work 46–49
empathy 42–43, 47
employment landscape, for professional musicians: employment *versus* underemployment 88–89; post-graduation path to employment 87–88
employment skill-building 94–97
enriched learning experiences 52
entrepreneurial culture 2
entrepreneurialism 10
entrepreneurship 5, 68–71, 76, 77, 81, 82
experience, building 19, 21

Floyd, G.: murder of 64, 99
Ford, H. 72
Frost Method®, The 95
Frost School, The 95

Gamebords 19
GAME of Innovation, The 2
Gatherables 18
Gear 18
global pandemic, effect on future generations of professional musicians 99–100
group improvisation 81–84

Harrington, C. 93, 98, 102n24
Haskins, D. 94, 96–97
heart work: in action 45–49; attributes of community and 51–53; emotional intelligence strategies in 46–49; openness of 42–43; as pedagogical approach 53–56
Herendeen, D. 96
hiring practices 32–33, 89–103, **91**
holistic education 98

IDEO Labs 8
Iino, R. 92, 97, 101

improvisation 8, 71, 73, 76, 78–80, 85, 97; collaborative 67, 68, 84; group 81–84
innovation 2, 3, 8, 10, 12
"Innovation GAME" design 13–35; additional opportunities 34–35; amplification 26–28; arena, establishment of 16–18; assessments 31–32; book club 32; culture statement 28–29; distinct value generator 25–26; experience, building 19, 21; guidelines, determination of 14–16; hiring practices 32–33; material selection 18–19; meetings 29–31; onboarding 33–34; professional development 31; Resource RETHINK 24; retreats 31; 75-Minute GAME 21–22
instrument-think 8–9
interdisciplinary collaboration 5
interpersonal communication 46, 48, 49
Israel, D. 90, 94, 98, 102n24

justice 40; social 58, 101

kindness 42
King, M. L., Jr. 40

lack of training 7–8
Ladson-Billings, G. 57
leadership 5; bottom-up 12–13; top-down 12–13
love 46, 47

Ma, Yo-Yo 101
material selection 18–19
Mayer, J. D. 47
meetings 29–31
mind work: in action 45–49; attributes of community and 51–53; emotional intelligence strategies in 46–49; openness of 43–45; as pedagogical approach 53–56
MIRA *see* Music Industry Research Association
misaligned incentives 9–11
mission statement 28

music, employment trends 86–101
music, future trends 99–100
musical excellence 3
music faculty 2, 8
musician's post-graduation path to employment 87–88
Music Industry Research Association (MIRA) 88, 89
music in higher education: changing 1–35
music schools: financial standing of 6; jury grading rubrics 92–93
music students, skills and perspectives of 2

National Endowment for the Arts (NEA) 88–89; "Artists and Other Cultural Workers: a Statistical Report" 88
NEA *see* National Endowment for the Arts
networking 97
note-taking 18

obstacles 23–24
O'Hara, K. 96, 102n19
onboarding 33–34

Peck, M. S. 39
Period 17
Place 17
playfulness 71, 77, 80
ponder time 78–79
Princeton University Survey Research Center 89
Prinz, L. 92, 97
private lessons 5
proactive communication 5
professional development 31, 94–97
Puzzlers 16–17

recruitment 4
relationships 52
reputation 4
resistance to truth-telling 40
Resource RETHINK 24
resources 5
retreats 31
revenue 4
Rules 29

Salovey, P. 47
scribing 18
self-accountability 45
self-care 46
self-compassion 42
self-development 46
self-examination 41, 45
self-improvement 45
self-reflection 45
service-learning 5
75-Minute GAME 21–22
shared values, honoring of 51–52
small class sizes 5
social justice 58, 101
solidarity 53
stage presence 93
strategic planning 69
student preparation 4
sustainability 5–6, 42, 49
SWOT diagrams 19
systemic obstacles, overcoming 6–13; bottom-up/top-down leadership 12–13; instrument-think 8–9; lack of training 7–8; misaligned incentives 9–11; upside-down faculty priorities 11–12
systemic racism 64

tax preparation 69
Team Time 19
tenure 10
Tenure and Promotion (T & P) guidelines 9, 10
top-down leadership 12–13
T & P *see* Tenure and Promotion guidelines
Traditions 29
transformational healing 58
transparency 52
"triple threat" artist 96
true community 39, 40
2018 Music Industry Research Association (MIRA) Survey of Musicians 99

underemployment *versus* employment 88–89
University of South Carolina (USC): entrepreneurship 5; obstacles, embracing 24
upside-down faculty priorities 11–12
USC *see* University of South Carolina

value 52–53
vignette videos 24
vulnerability 42

Wade, C. 55
willful participation 52